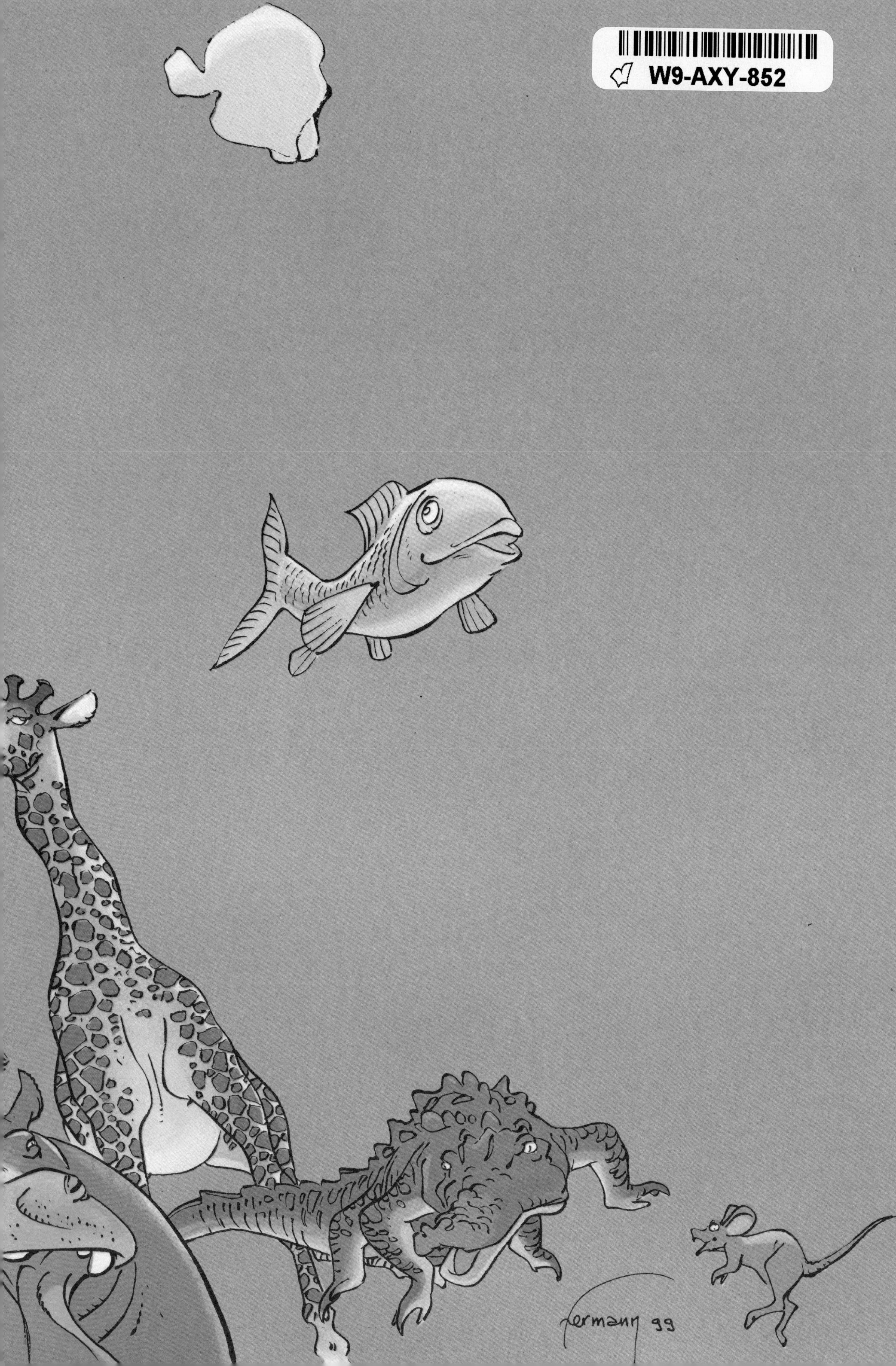

HEY, NICK! ARE YOU DREAMING?

Hermann

Script: Morphée

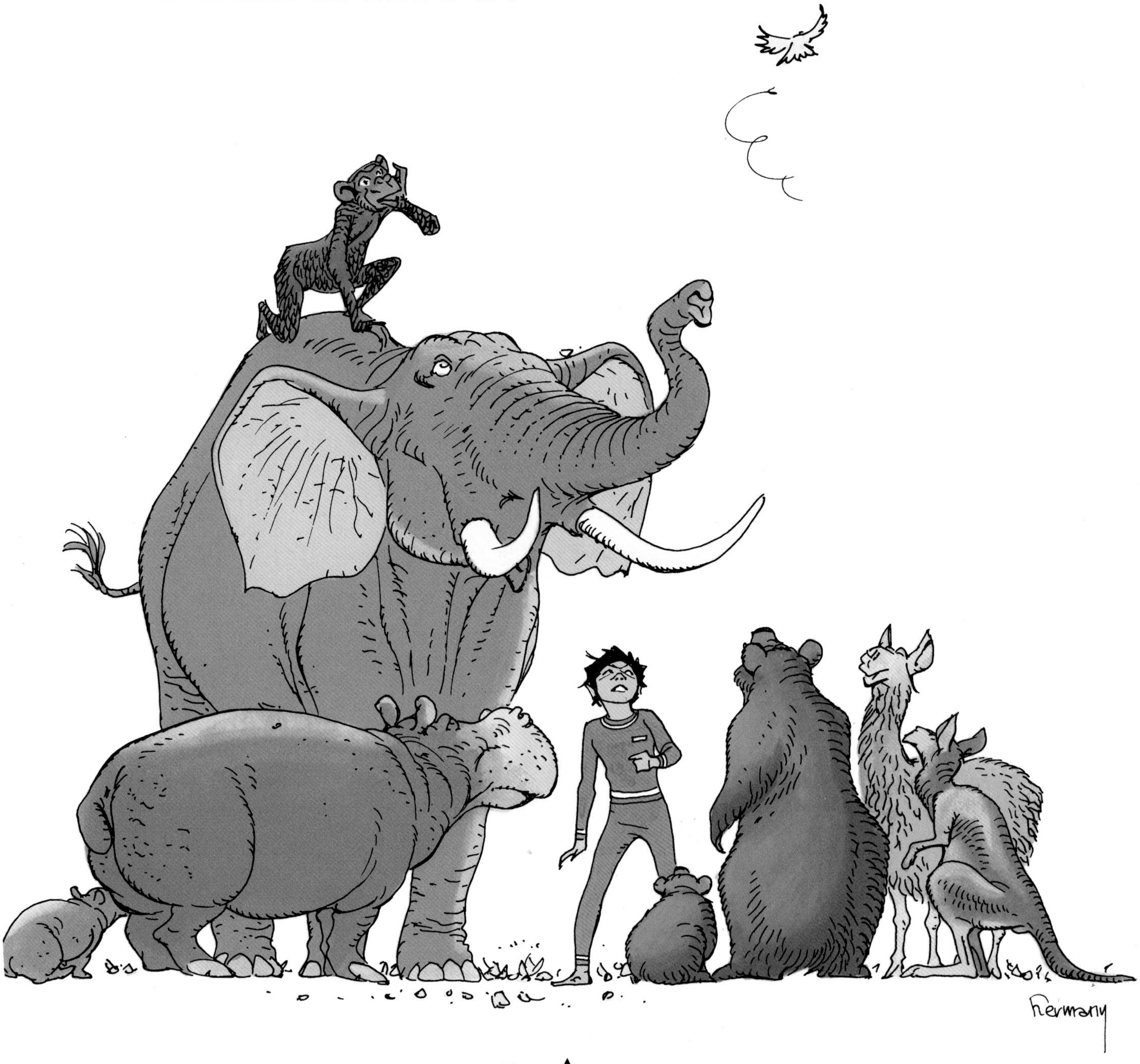

SAF COMICS

Dreams are the aquarium of the night.

Victor Hugo

Hermann • Morphée

HEY, NICK! ARE YOU DREAMING?

© Strip Art Features, 2004. All rights reserved.

Editorial office:

SAF COMICS
Krpanova 1, 3000 Celje, Slovenia
Tel. (386-3) 425-0500
Fax: (386-3) 545-1774

www.safcomics.com
info@safcomics.com

First edition: January 2004
ISBN: 1-59396-015-8

Printed in Slovenia by SAF - Tiskarna Koper

DREAM CHAPTER 1
STRANGE CAPTAIN BANG

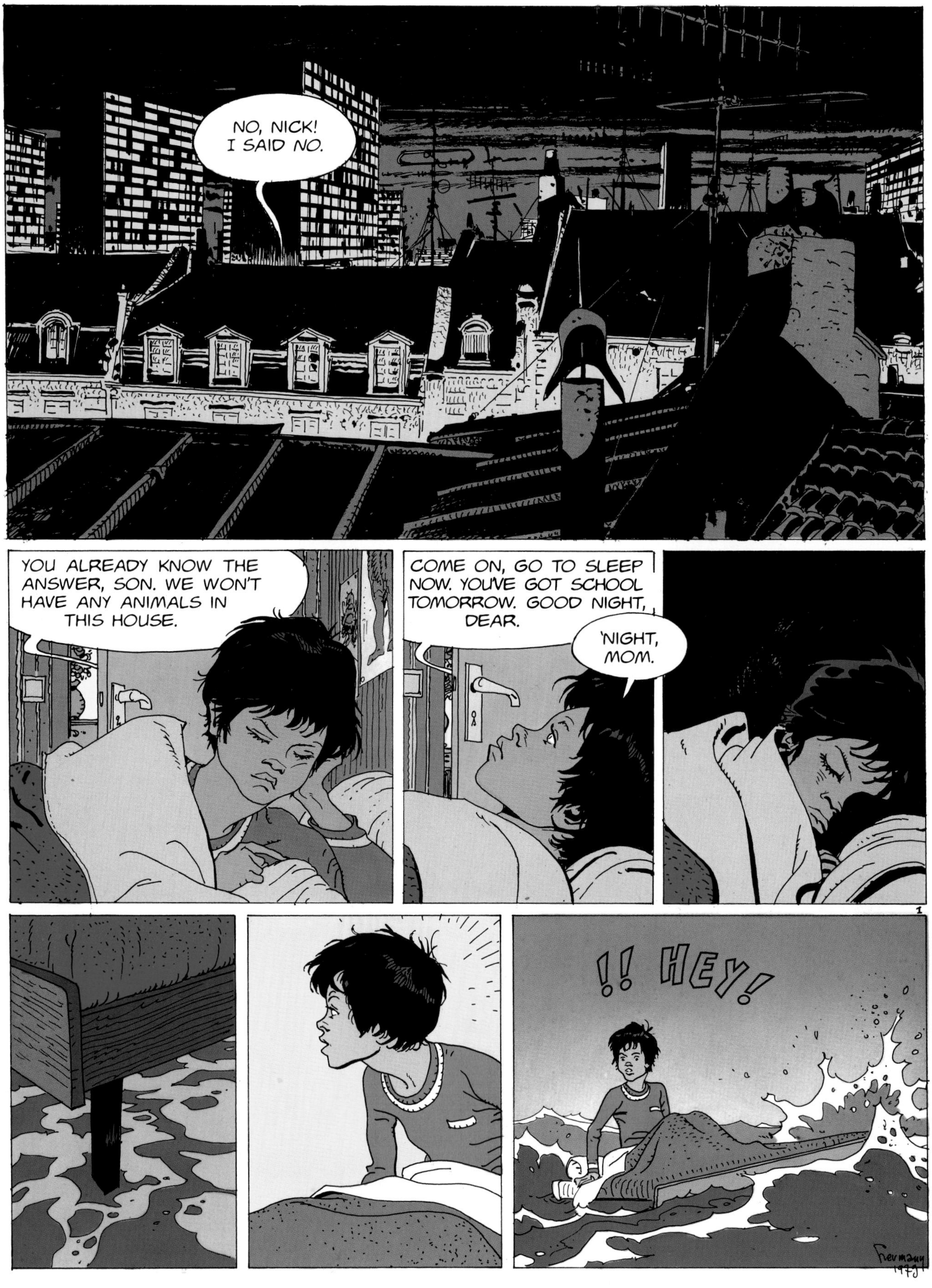
NO, NICK! I SAID NO.
YOU ALREADY KNOW THE ANSWER, SON. WE WON'T HAVE ANY ANIMALS IN THIS HOUSE.
COME ON, GO TO SLEEP NOW. YOU'VE GOT SCHOOL TOMORROW. GOOD NIGHT, DEAR.
'NIGHT, MOM.
!! HEY!
Hermann 1973

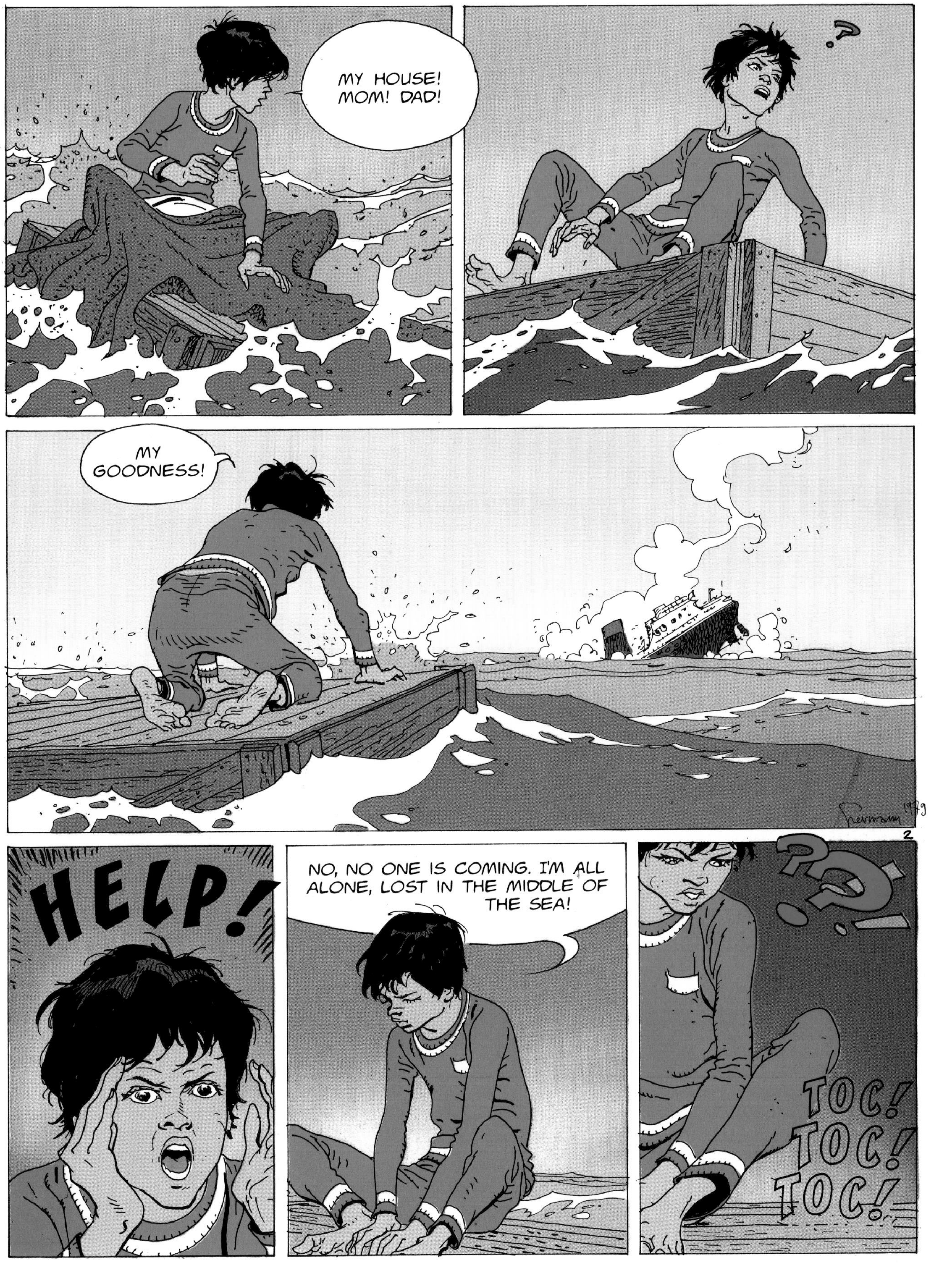
MY HOUSE! MOM! DAD!
?
MY GOODNESS!
HELP!
NO, NO ONE IS COMING. I'M ALL ALONE, LOST IN THE MIDDLE OF THE SEA!
??!
TOC! TOC! TOC!

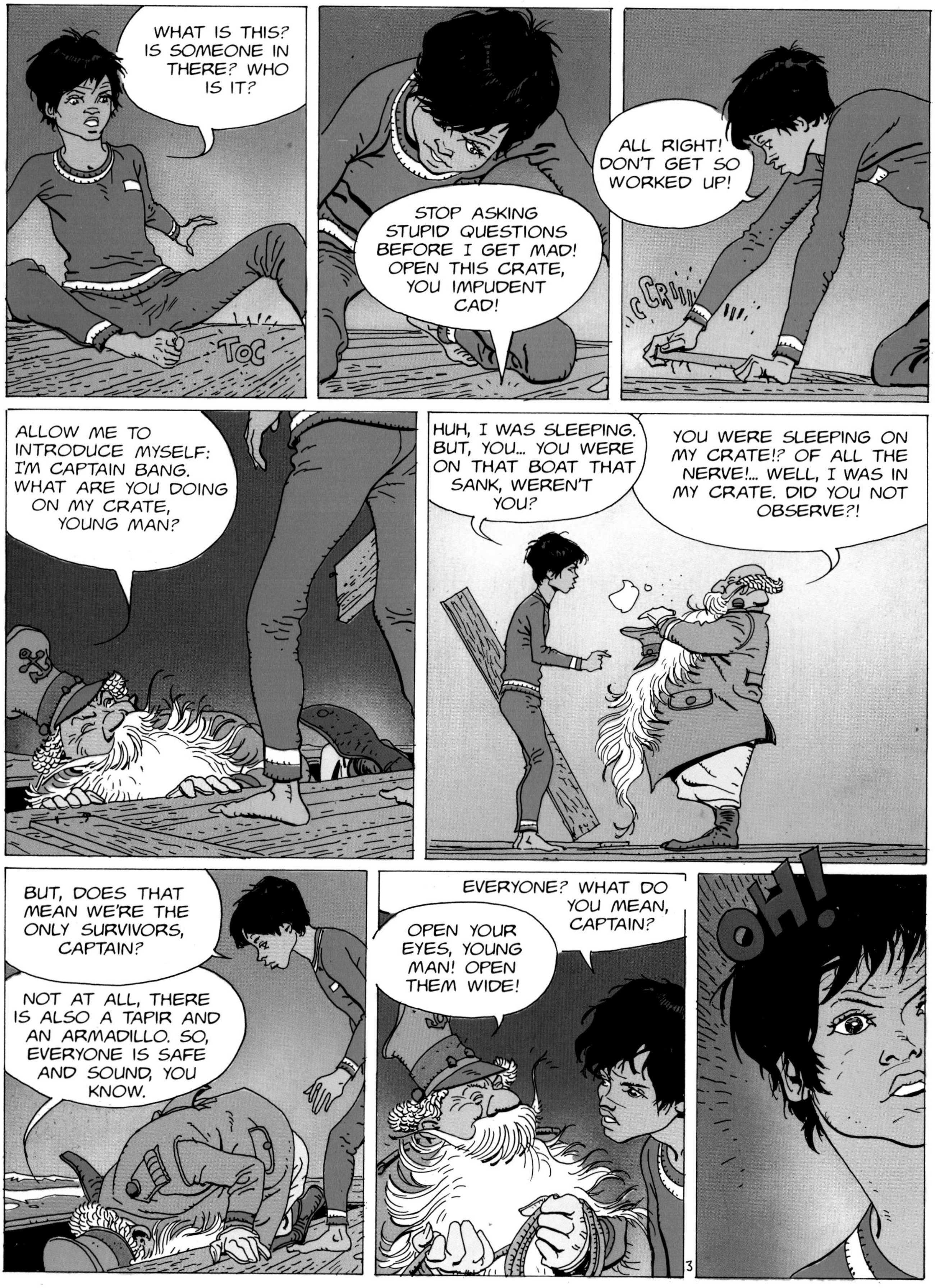
WHAT IS THIS? IS SOMEONE IN THERE? WHO IS IT?
TOC
STOP ASKING STUPID QUESTIONS BEFORE I GET MAD! OPEN THIS CRATE, YOU IMPUDENT CAD!
ALL RIGHT! DON'T GET SO WORKED UP!
CCRIIII
ALLOW ME TO INTRODUCE MYSELF: I'M CAPTAIN BANG. WHAT ARE YOU DOING ON MY CRATE, YOUNG MAN?
HUH, I WAS SLEEPING. BUT, YOU... YOU WERE ON THAT BOAT THAT SANK, WEREN'T YOU?
YOU WERE SLEEPING ON MY CRATE!? OF ALL THE NERVE!... WELL, I WAS IN MY CRATE. DID YOU NOT OBSERVE?!
BUT, DOES THAT MEAN WE'RE THE ONLY SURVIVORS, CAPTAIN?
NOT AT ALL, THERE IS ALSO A TAPIR AND AN ARMADILLO. SO, EVERYONE IS SAFE AND SOUND, YOU KNOW.
EVERYONE? WHAT DO YOU MEAN, CAPTAIN?
OPEN YOUR EYES, YOUNG MAN! OPEN THEM WIDE!
OH!
3

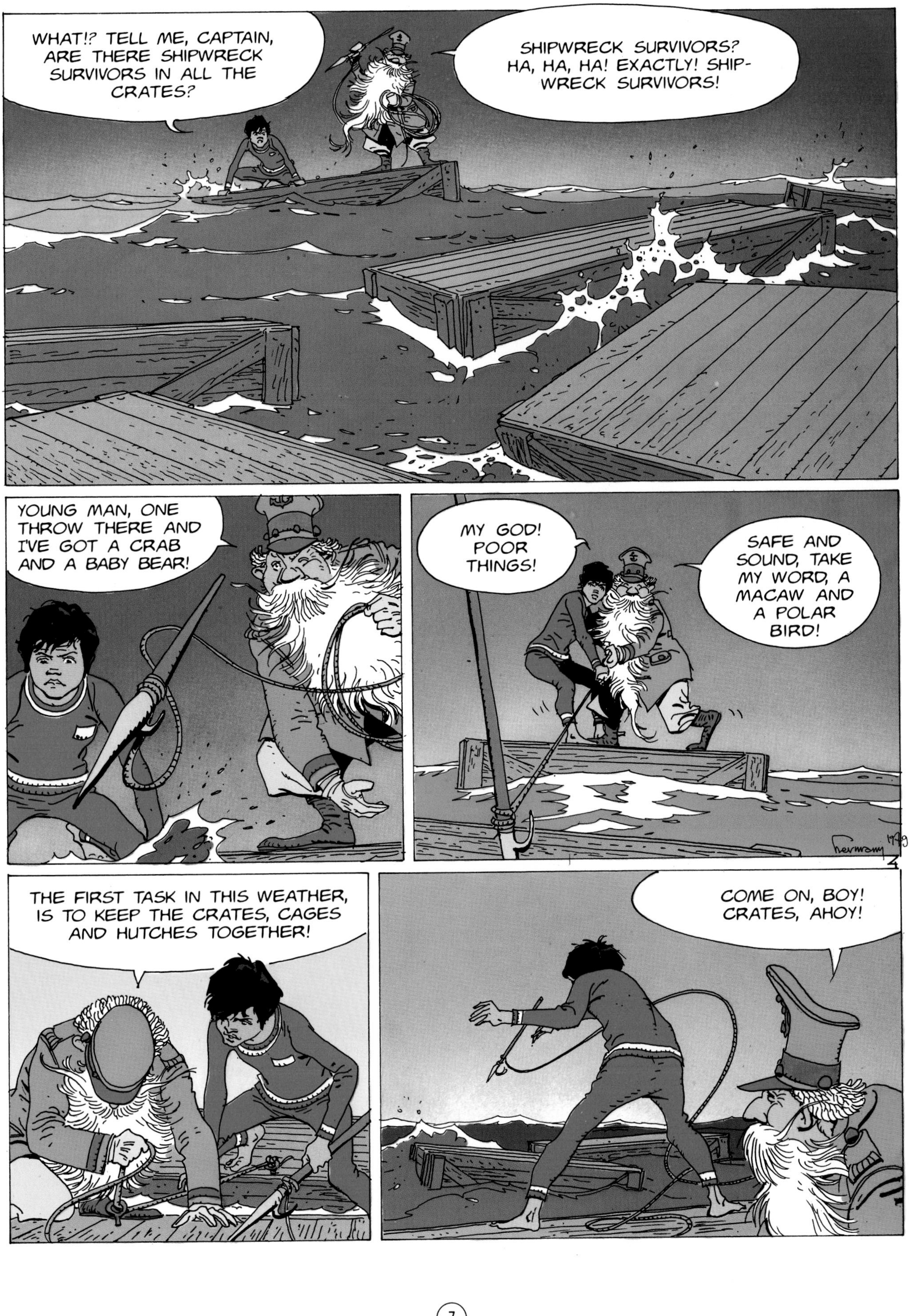
WHAT!? TELL ME, CAPTAIN, ARE THERE SHIPWRECK SURVIVORS IN ALL THE CRATES?
SHIPWRECK SURVIVORS? HA, HA, HA! EXACTLY! SHIP-WRECK SURVIVORS!
YOUNG MAN, ONE THROW THERE AND I'VE GOT A CRAB AND A BABY BEAR!
MY GOD! POOR THINGS!
SAFE AND SOUND, TAKE MY WORD, A MACAW AND A POLAR BIRD!
THE FIRST TASK IN THIS WEATHER, IS TO KEEP THE CRATES, CAGES AND HUTCHES TOGETHER!
COME ON, BOY! CRATES, AHOY!

NICE JOB, YOUNG MAN! JOLLY NICE!

MAYBE WE COULD OPEN THE CRATES NOW?

GILLS AND WHALEBONES! DON'T TOUCH A THING! HELP ME...

...PUT THIS IN THE WATER. RAVEN DROPPINGS!

YOU LIKE SPORTS, YOUNG MAN?

WELL, AHEM... YES, CAPTAIN. BUT... WHAT ABOUT THE SURVIVORS?

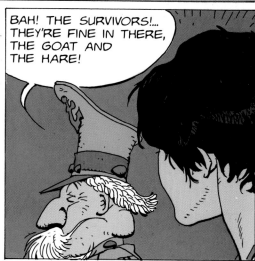

BAH! THE SURVIVORS!... THEY'RE FINE IN THERE, THE GOAT AND THE HARE!

LET'S SEE, CAPTAIN, YOU CAN'T BE SERIOUS!?! GOATS AND HARES!

HM... BUT, I AM, I AM.

IF IT'S LIKE THIS, I'LL OPEN THE CRATES MYSELF!

FINE... GO AHEAD!

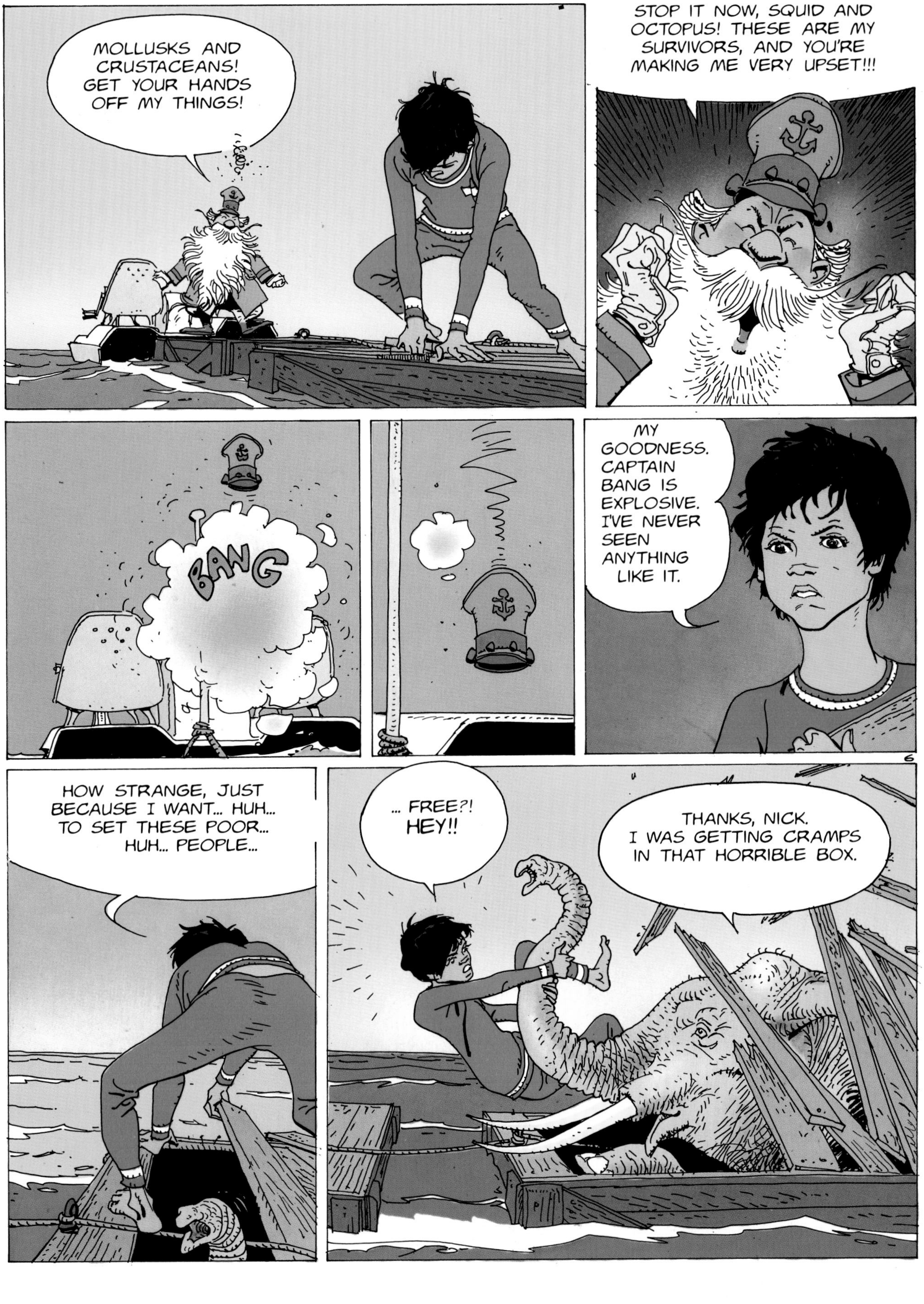
MOLLUSKS AND CRUSTACEANS! GET YOUR HANDS OFF MY THINGS!
STOP IT NOW, SQUID AND OCTOPUS! THESE ARE MY SURVIVORS, AND YOU'RE MAKING ME VERY UPSET!!!
BANG
MY GOODNESS. CAPTAIN BANG IS EXPLOSIVE. I'VE NEVER SEEN ANYTHING LIKE IT.
HOW STRANGE, JUST BECAUSE I WANT... HUH... TO SET THESE POOR... HUH... PEOPLE...
... FREE?! HEY!!
THANKS, NICK. I WAS GETTING CRAMPS IN THAT HORRIBLE BOX.

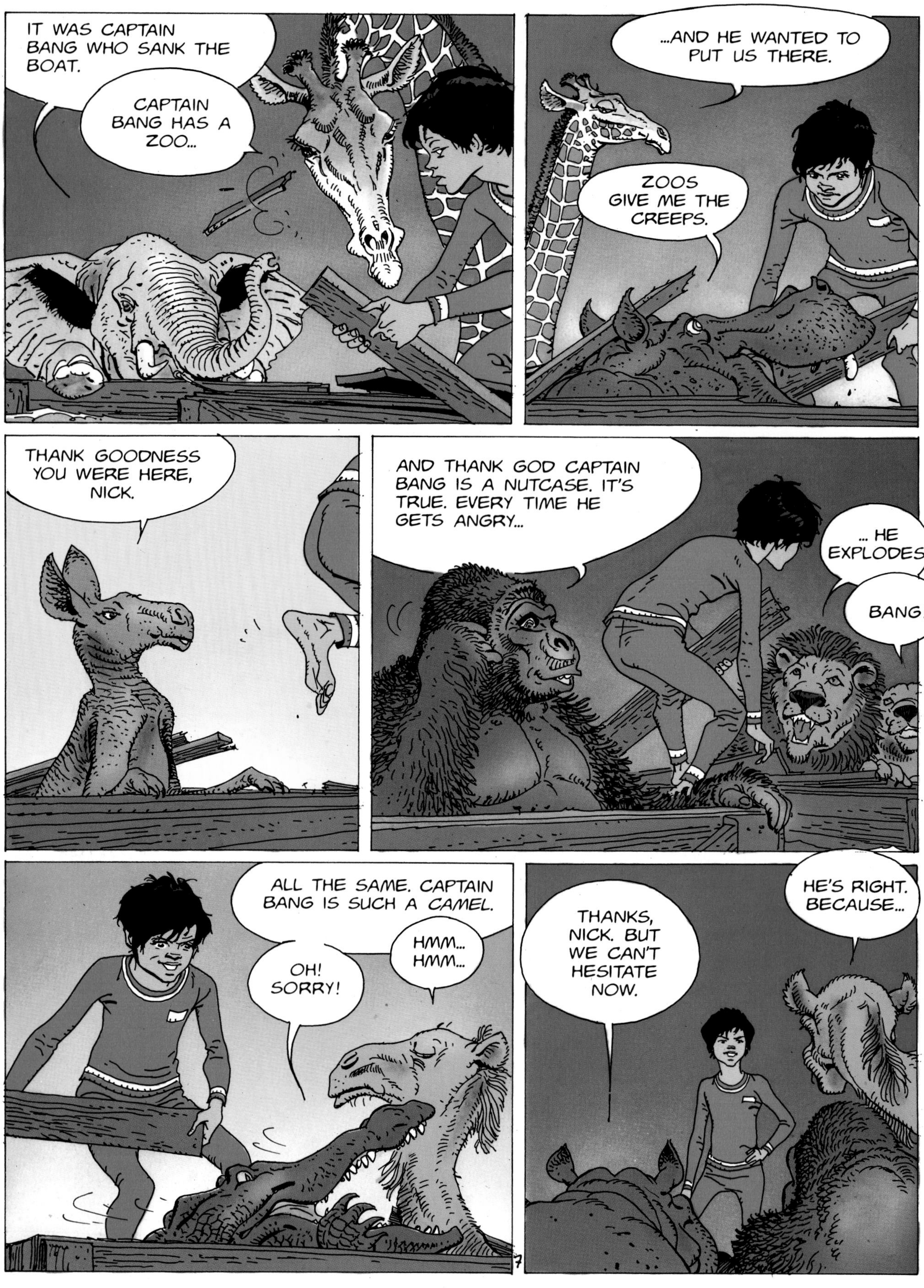
IT WAS CAPTAIN BANG WHO SANK THE BOAT.
CAPTAIN BANG HAS A ZOO...
...AND HE WANTED TO PUT US THERE.
ZOOS GIVE ME THE CREEPS.
THANK GOODNESS YOU WERE HERE, NICK.
AND THANK GOD CAPTAIN BANG IS A NUTCASE. IT'S TRUE. EVERY TIME HE GETS ANGRY...
... HE EXPLODES.
BANG!
ALL THE SAME. CAPTAIN BANG IS SUCH A CAMEL.
OH! SORRY!
HMM... HMM...
THANKS, NICK. BUT WE CAN'T HESITATE NOW.
HE'S RIGHT. BECAUSE...

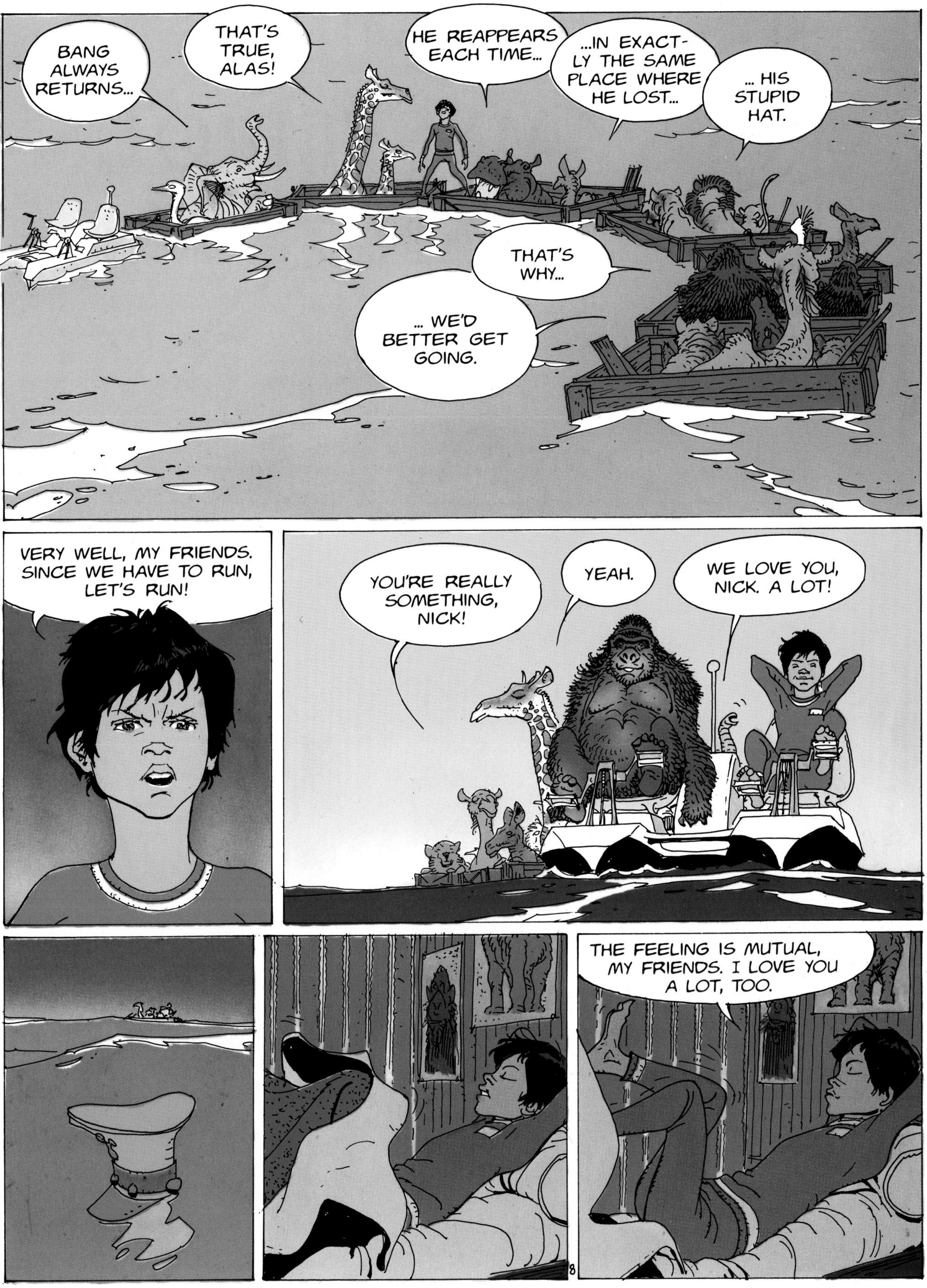
BANG ALWAYS RETURNS...
THAT'S TRUE, ALAS!
HE REAPPEARS EACH TIME...
...IN EXACT-LY THE SAME PLACE WHERE HE LOST...
... HIS STUPID HAT.
THAT'S WHY...
... WE'D BETTER GET GOING.
VERY WELL, MY FRIENDS. SINCE WE HAVE TO RUN, LET'S RUN!
YOU'RE REALLY SOMETHING, NICK!
YEAH.
WE LOVE YOU, NICK. A LOT!
THE FEELING IS MUTUAL, MY FRIENDS. I LOVE YOU A LOT, TOO.

DREAM CHAPTER 2

A VERY MYSTERIOUS ISLAND

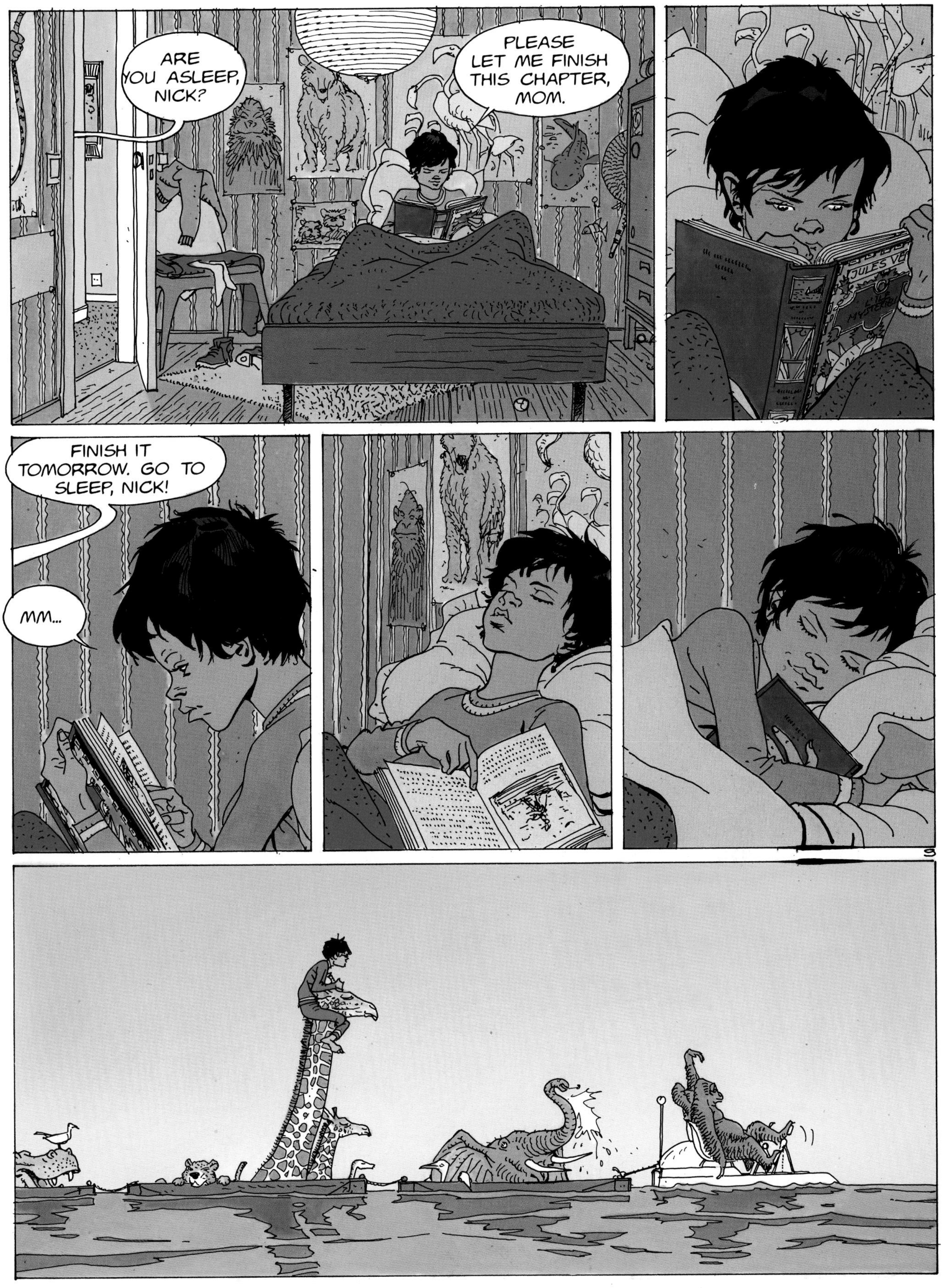
ARE YOU ASLEEP, NICK?
PLEASE LET ME FINISH THIS CHAPTER, MOM.
FINISH IT TOMORROW. GO TO SLEEP, NICK!
MM...

LAND AHOY, MATEYS! I SEE AN ISLAND!... NO, TWO ISLANDS!

THAT'S RIGHT, FOLKS!

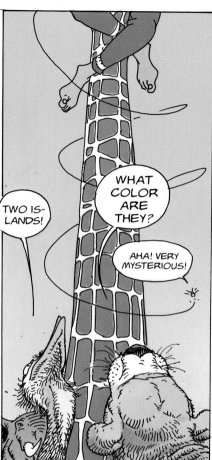

TWO IS-LANDS!

WHAT COLOR ARE THEY?

AHA! VERY MYSTERIOUS!

ONE OF THEM IS BLACK.

AS BLACK AS COAL.

A BLACK ISLAND.

HOW SAD.

AND THE OTHER?

IT IS PINK.

LIKE A RADISH!

MAGNIFICENT!

A PINK ISLAND!

LET'S GO!

ON YOUR WAY, ALPHONSE!

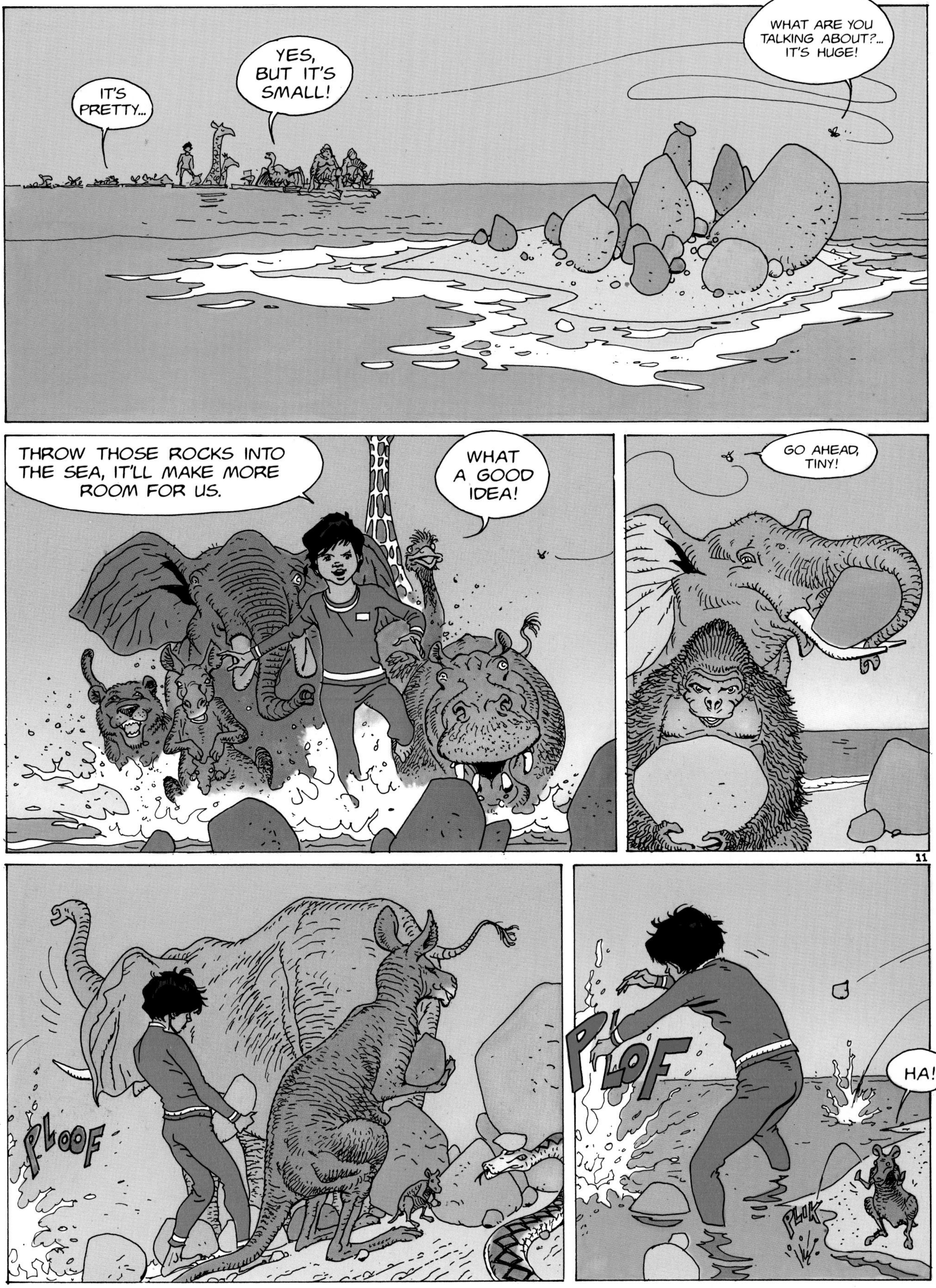
IT'S PRETTY...
YES, BUT IT'S SMALL!
WHAT ARE YOU TALKING ABOUT?... IT'S HUGE!
THROW THOSE ROCKS INTO THE SEA, IT'LL MAKE MORE ROOM FOR US.
WHAT A GOOD IDEA!
GO AHEAD, TINY!
11
PLOOF
PLOF
HA!
PLIK

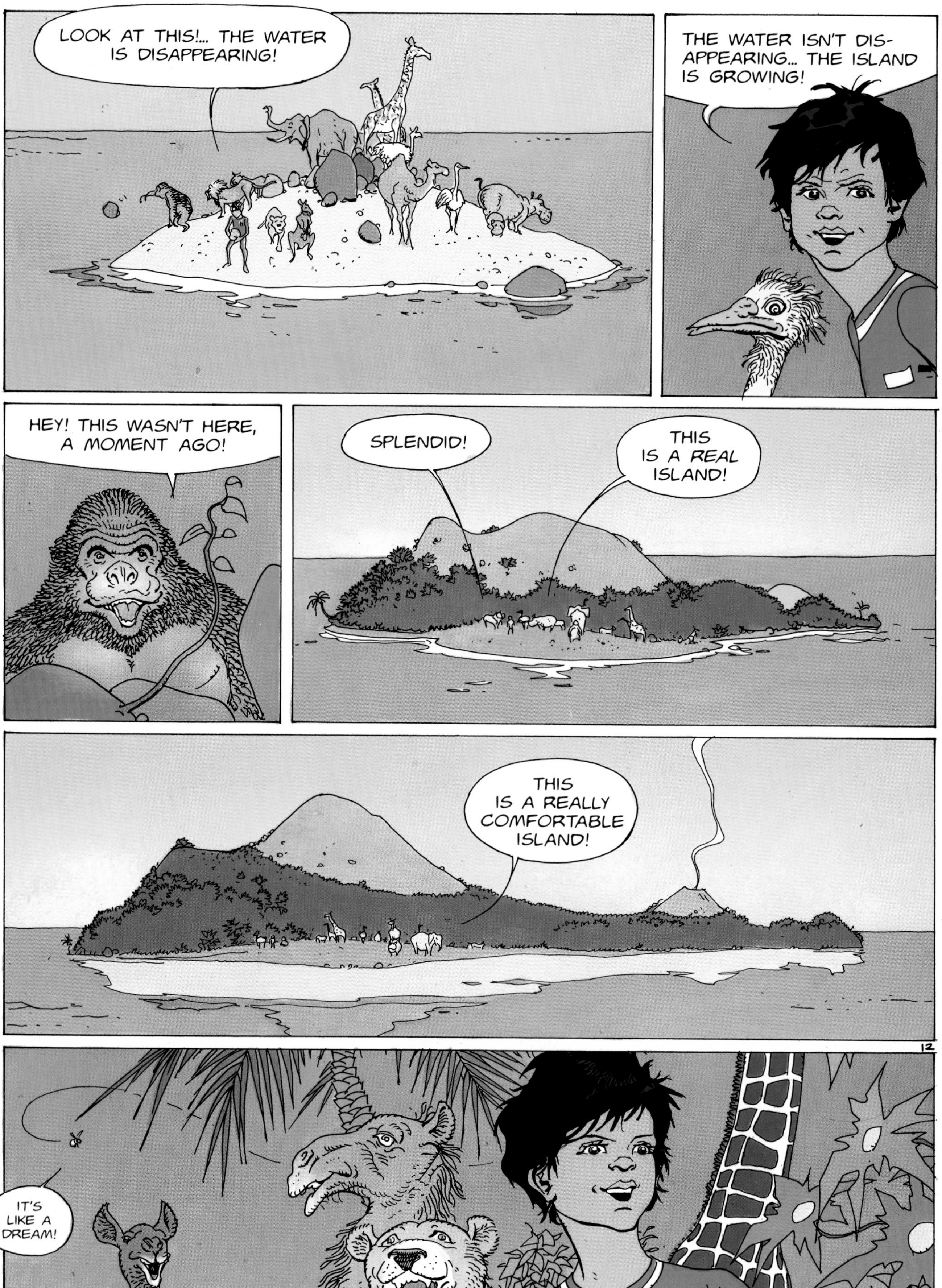

LOOK AT THIS!... THE WATER IS DISAPPEARING!
THE WATER ISN'T DISAPPEARING... THE ISLAND IS GROWING!
HEY! THIS WASN'T HERE, A MOMENT AGO!
SPLENDID!
THIS IS A REAL ISLAND!
THIS IS A REALLY COMFORTABLE ISLAND!
12
IT'S LIKE A DREAM!

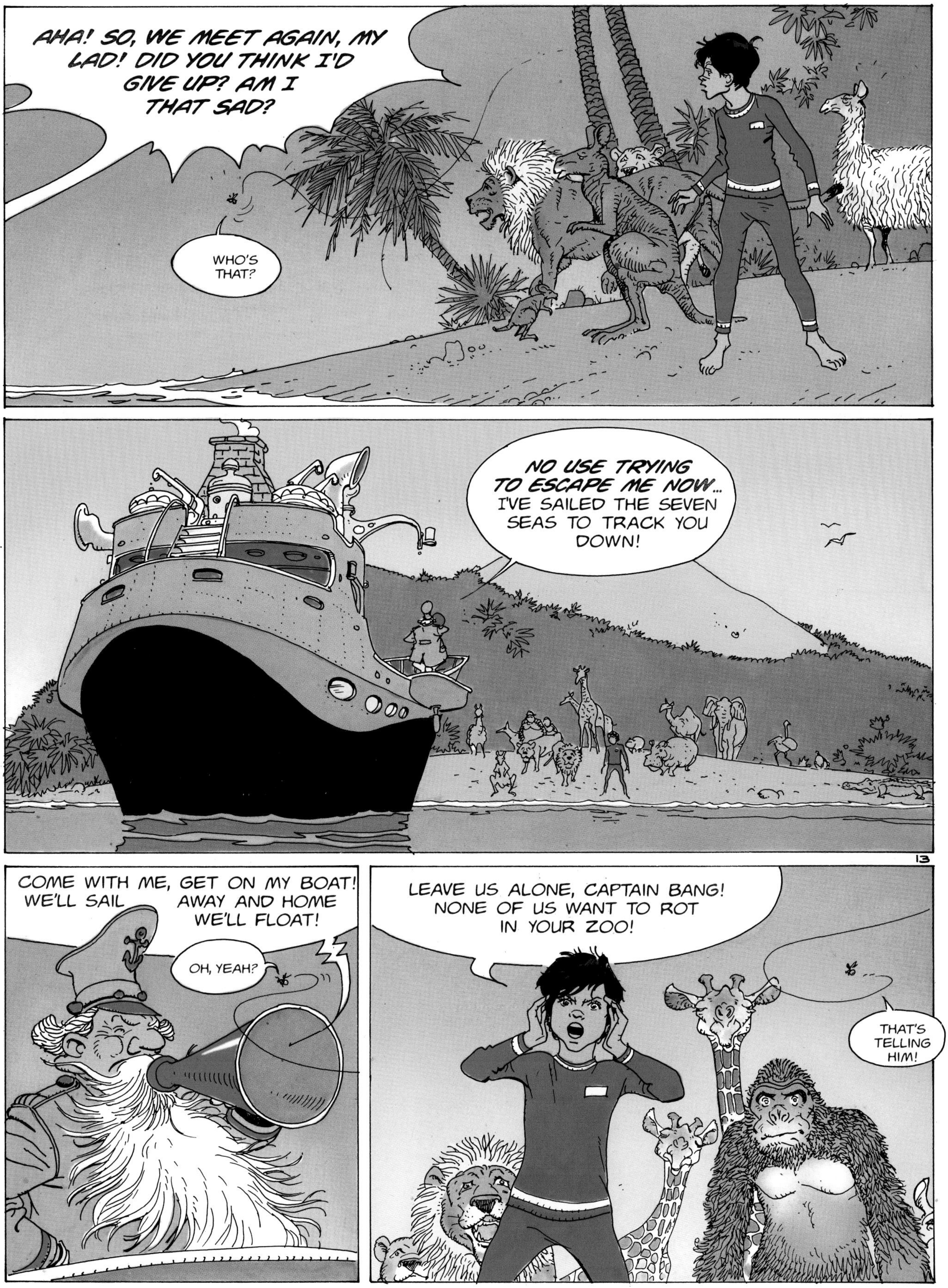
AHA! SO, WE MEET AGAIN, MY LAD! DID YOU THINK I'D GIVE UP? AM I THAT SAD?
WHO'S THAT?
NO USE TRYING TO ESCAPE ME NOW... I'VE SAILED THE SEVEN SEAS TO TRACK YOU DOWN!
13
COME WITH ME, GET ON MY BOAT! WE'LL SAIL AWAY AND HOME WE'LL FLOAT!
OH, YEAH?
LEAVE US ALONE, CAPTAIN BANG! NONE OF US WANT TO ROT IN YOUR ZOO!
THAT'S TELLING HIM!

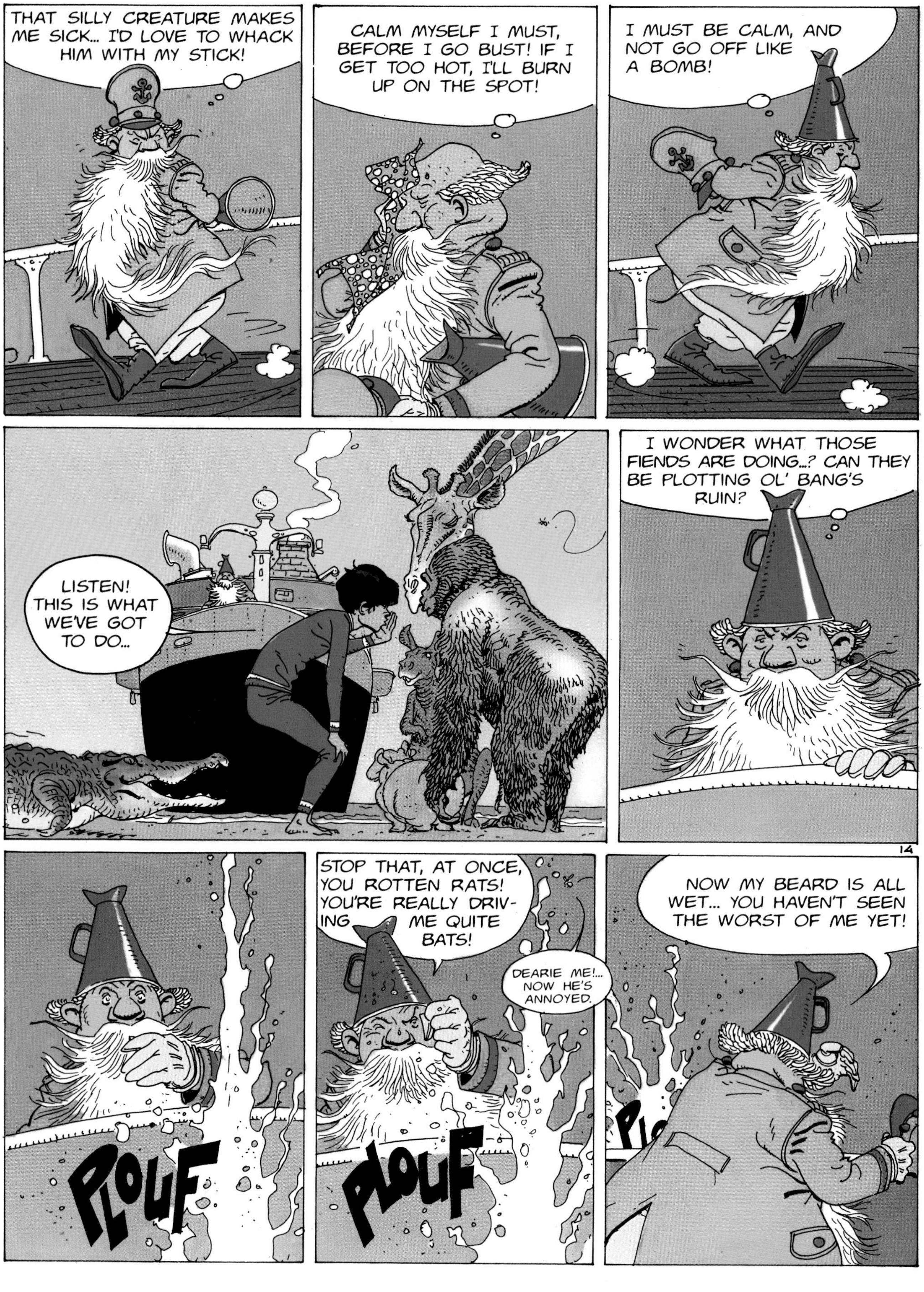
THAT SILLY CREATURE MAKES ME SICK... I'D LOVE TO WHACK HIM WITH MY STICK!
CALM MYSELF I MUST, BEFORE I GO BUST! IF I GET TOO HOT, I'LL BURN UP ON THE SPOT!
I MUST BE CALM, AND NOT GO OFF LIKE A BOMB!
LISTEN! THIS IS WHAT WE'VE GOT TO DO...
I WONDER WHAT THOSE FIENDS ARE DOING...? CAN THEY BE PLOTTING OL' BANG'S RUIN?
14
PLOUF
STOP THAT, AT ONCE, YOU ROTTEN RATS! YOU'RE REALLY DRIVING ME QUITE BATS!
DEARIE ME!... NOW HE'S ANNOYED.
PLOUF
NOW MY BEARD IS ALL WET... YOU HAVEN'T SEEN THE WORST OF ME YET!
PLO

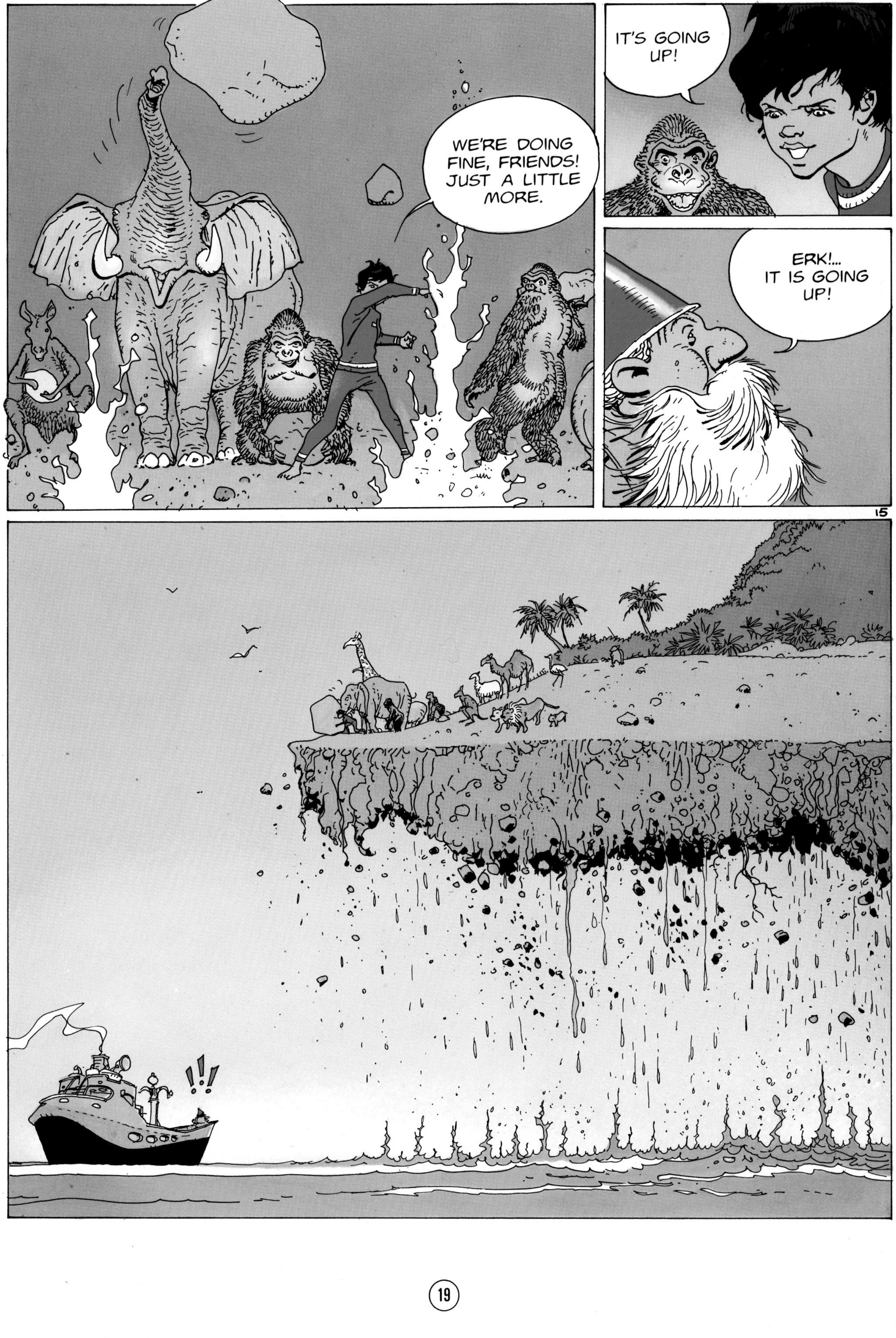
WE'RE DOING FINE, FRIENDS! JUST A LITTLE MORE.
IT'S GOING UP!
ERK!... IT IS GOING UP!
!!!

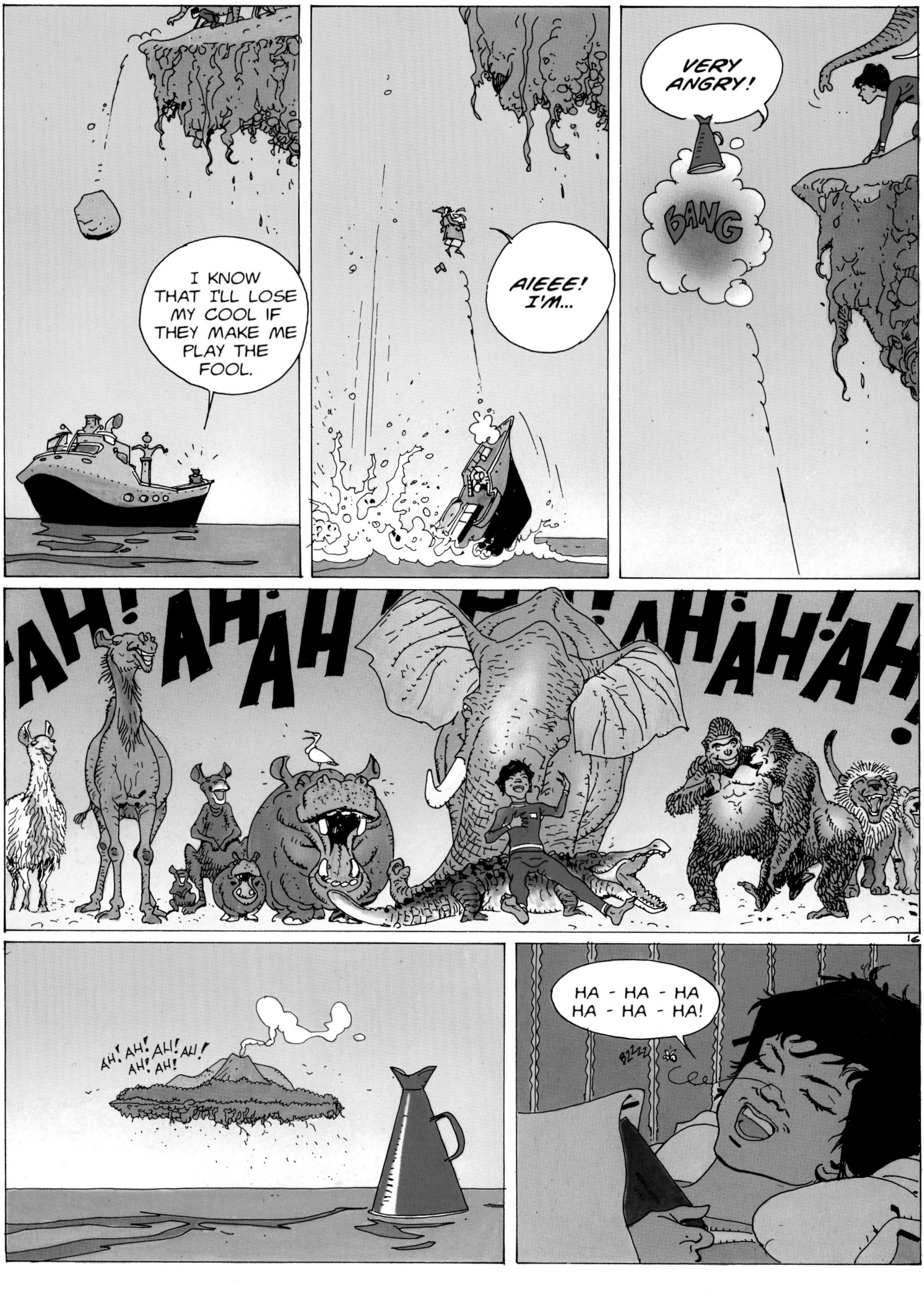
I KNOW THAT I'LL LOSE MY COOL IF THEY MAKE ME PLAY THE FOOL.
AIEEE! I'M...
VERY ANGRY!
BANG
AH! AH AH AH AH! AH! AH! AH! AH!
AH! AH! AH! AH! AH! AH!
HA - HA - HA HA - HA - HA!
BZZZ

DREAM CHAPTER 3

IN THE MEMORY OF LITTLE NEMO*

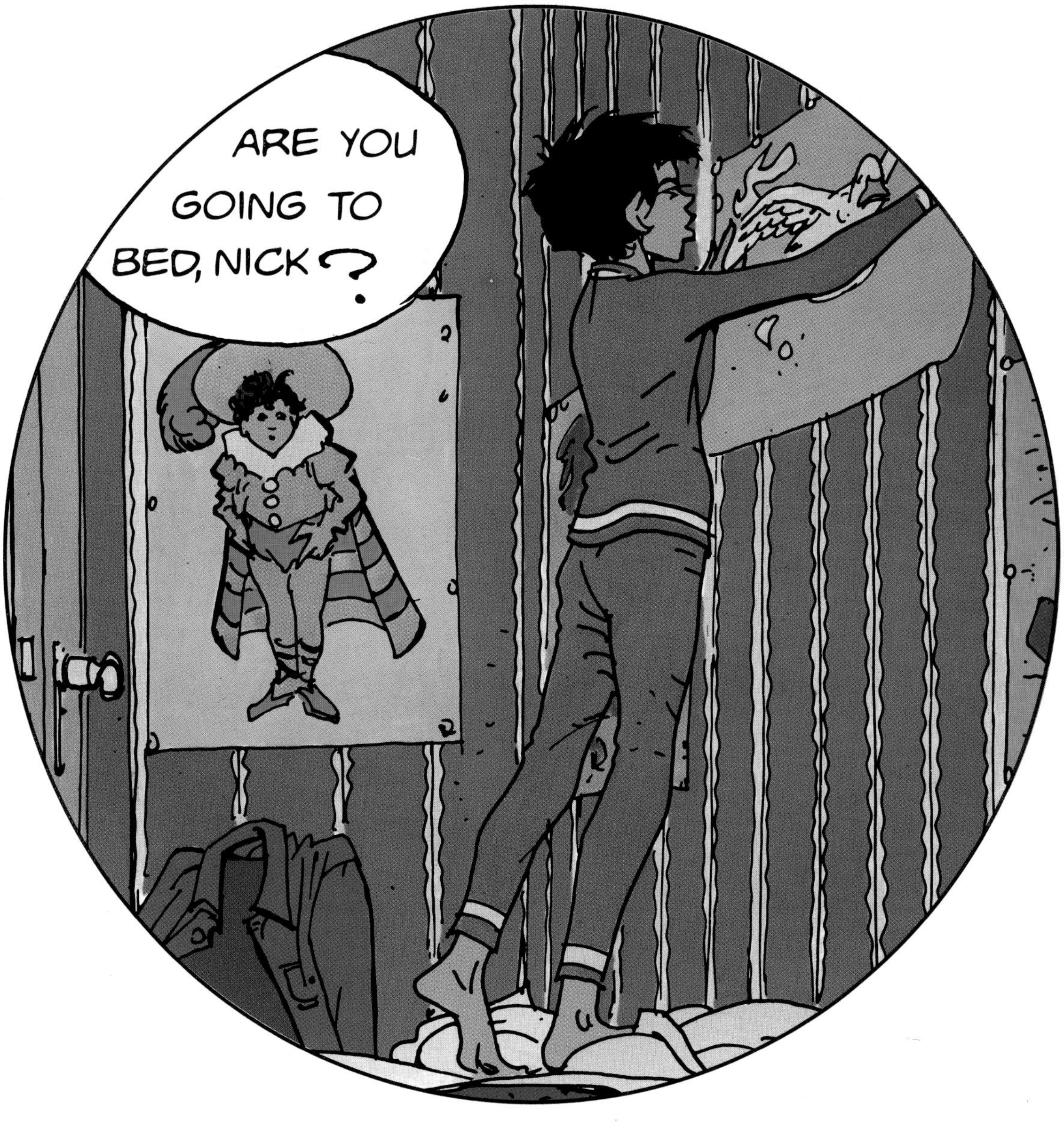
ARE YOU GOING TO BED, NICK?

*An homage to Windsor McCay (1869-1934), the brilliant creator of Little Nemo - Prince of Dreams in Images - a character seen on a poster in Nick's room.

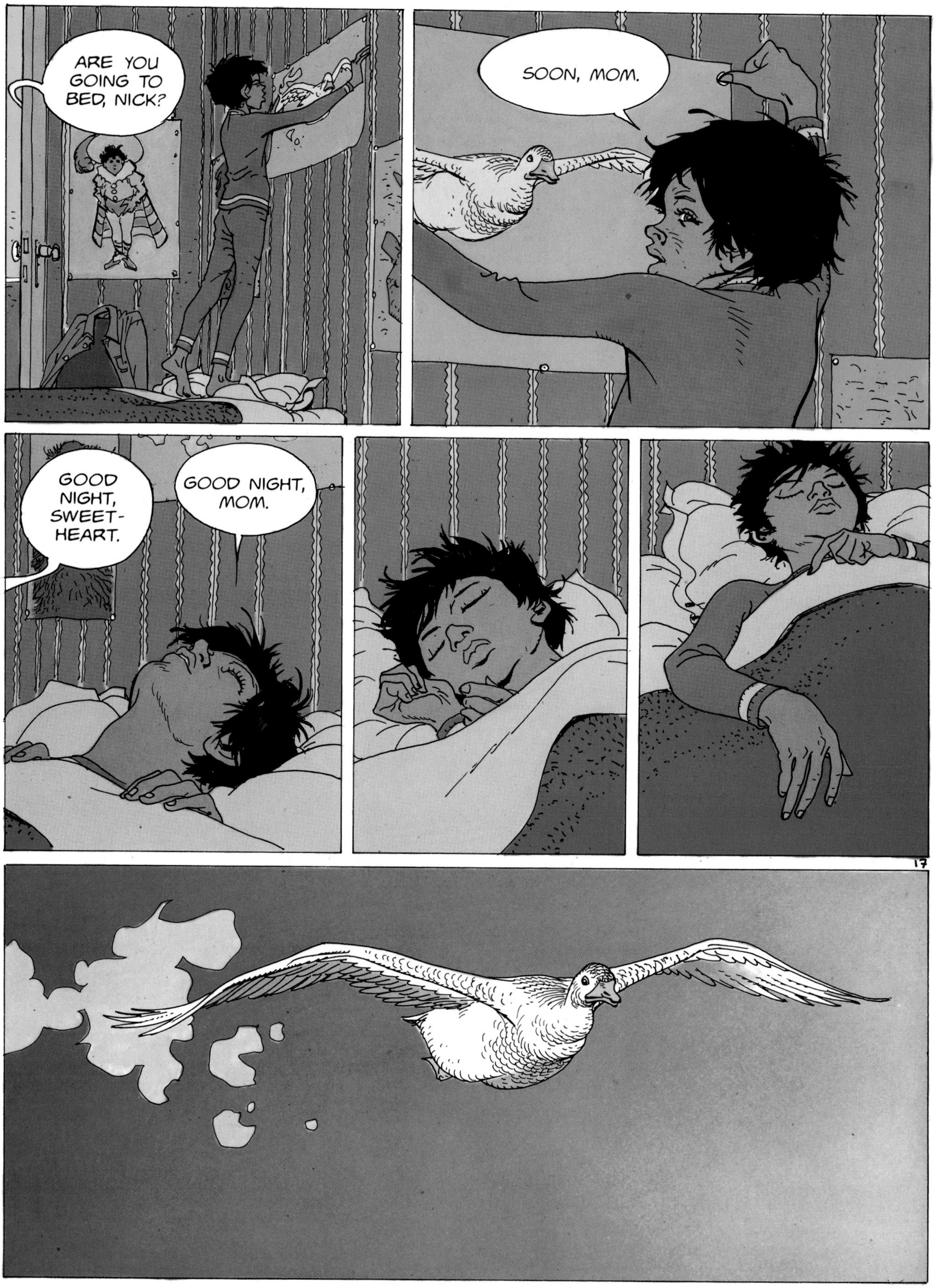
ARE YOU GOING TO BED, NICK?
SOON, MOM.
GOOD NIGHT, SWEET-HEART.
GOOD NIGHT, MOM.

PHEW! IT'S SO NICE TO CATCH MY BREATH FOR A WHILE!

HELLO!

HELLO... BUT, TELL ME...

18

HAVE YOU BY ANY CHANCE SEEN A SMALL, BEARDED, QUICK-TEMPERED OLD MAN?

MY GOODNESS! HOW DID YOU KNOW, ARE YOU SOME KIND OF MAGICIAN?

IN FACT, CAPTAIN BANG AND I WERE FLYING TOGETHER FOR A WHILE...

FLYING!?

FLYING?

FLYING?

FLYING?

FLYING?

!?!!

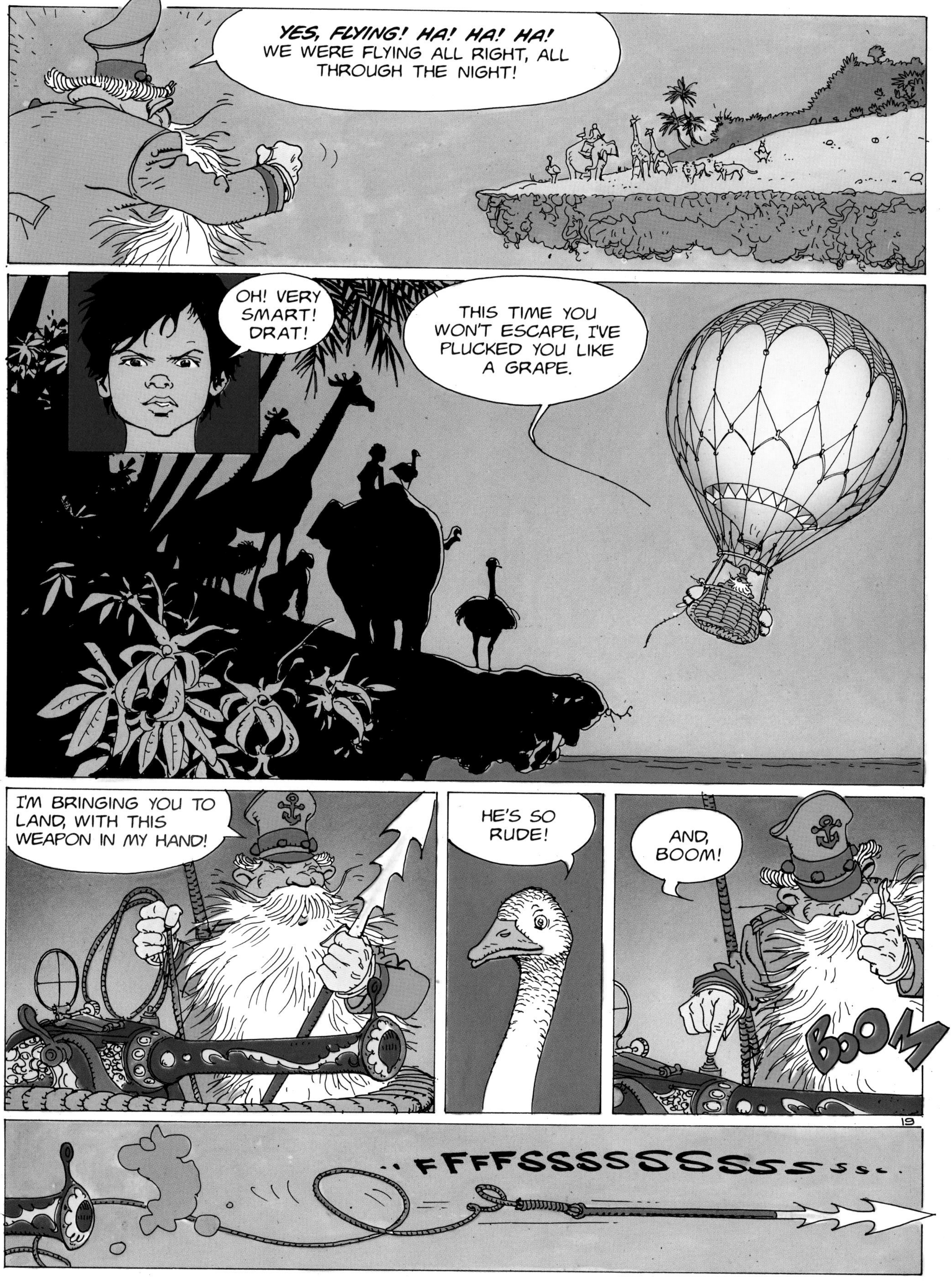
YES, FLYING! HA! HA! HA! WE WERE FLYING ALL RIGHT, ALL THROUGH THE NIGHT!
OH! VERY SMART! DRAT!
THIS TIME YOU WON'T ESCAPE, I'VE PLUCKED YOU LIKE A GRAPE.
I'M BRINGING YOU TO LAND, WITH THIS WEAPON IN MY HAND!
HE'S SO RUDE!
AND, BOOM!
BOOM
..FFFSSSSSSSSSSsss..

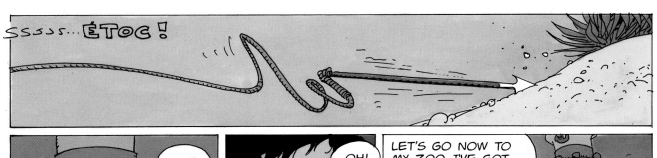

SSSSS... ÉTOC !

AH!

OH!

LET'S GO NOW TO MY ZOO, I'VE GOT SPACE FOR ALL OF YOU.

BUT... THAT SINISTER MAN IS KIDNAPPING US.

20

WE SIMPLY WON'T ALLOW IT... HUMPF...

LET'S PULL TOGETHER! HOP!

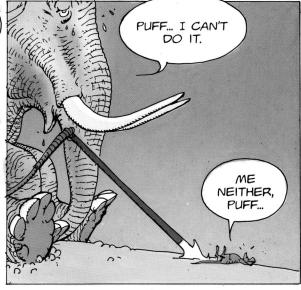

PUFF... I CAN'T DO IT.

ME NEITHER, PUFF...

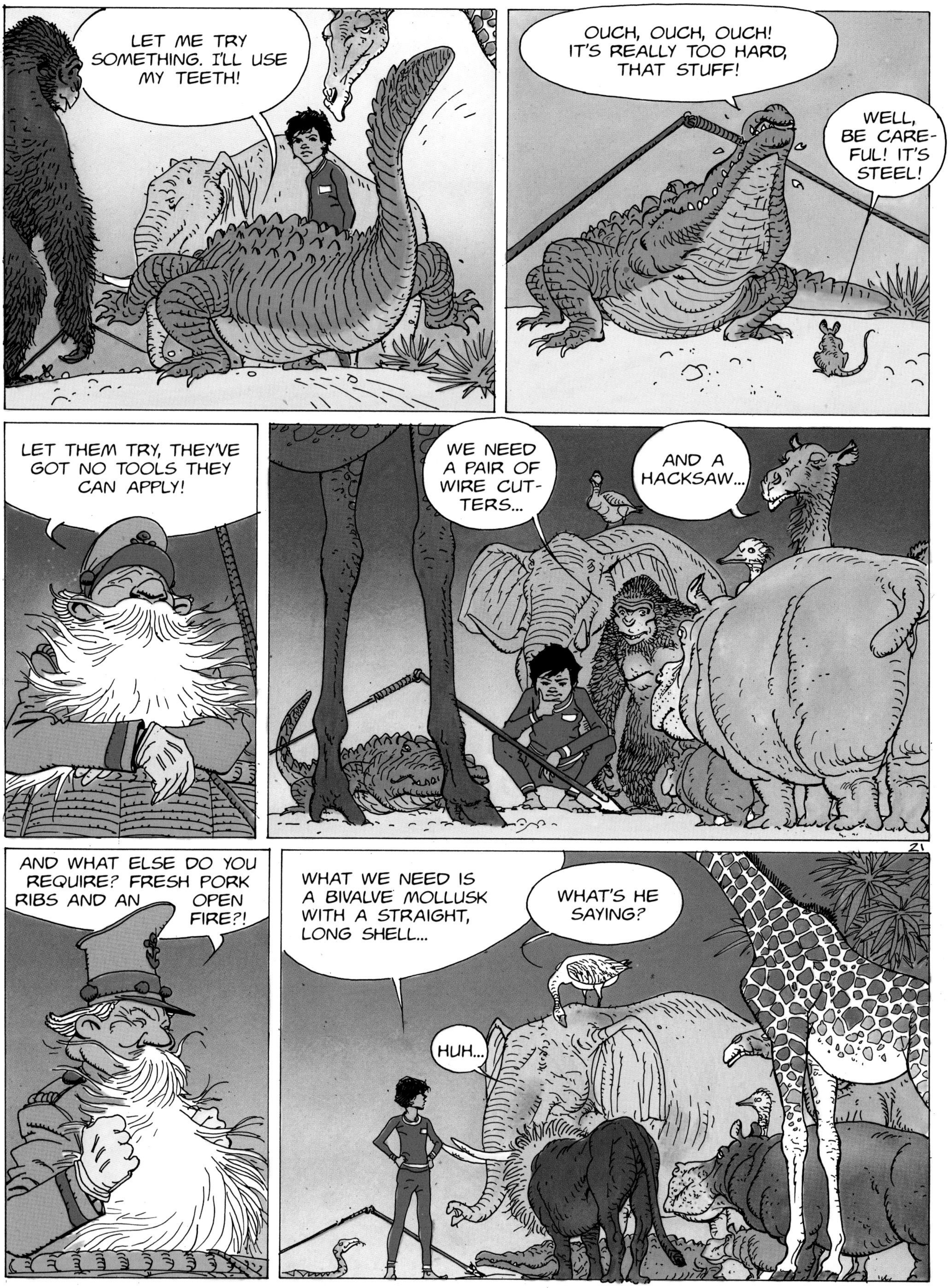
LET ME TRY SOMETHING. I'LL USE MY TEETH!
OUCH, OUCH, OUCH! IT'S REALLY TOO HARD, THAT STUFF!
WELL, BE CARE-FUL! IT'S STEEL!
LET THEM TRY, THEY'VE GOT NO TOOLS THEY CAN APPLY!
WE NEED A PAIR OF WIRE CUT-TERS...
AND A HACKSAW...
AND WHAT ELSE DO YOU REQUIRE? FRESH PORK RIBS AND AN OPEN FIRE?!
WHAT WE NEED IS A BIVALVE MOLLUSK WITH A STRAIGHT, LONG SHELL...
WHAT'S HE SAYING?
HUH...

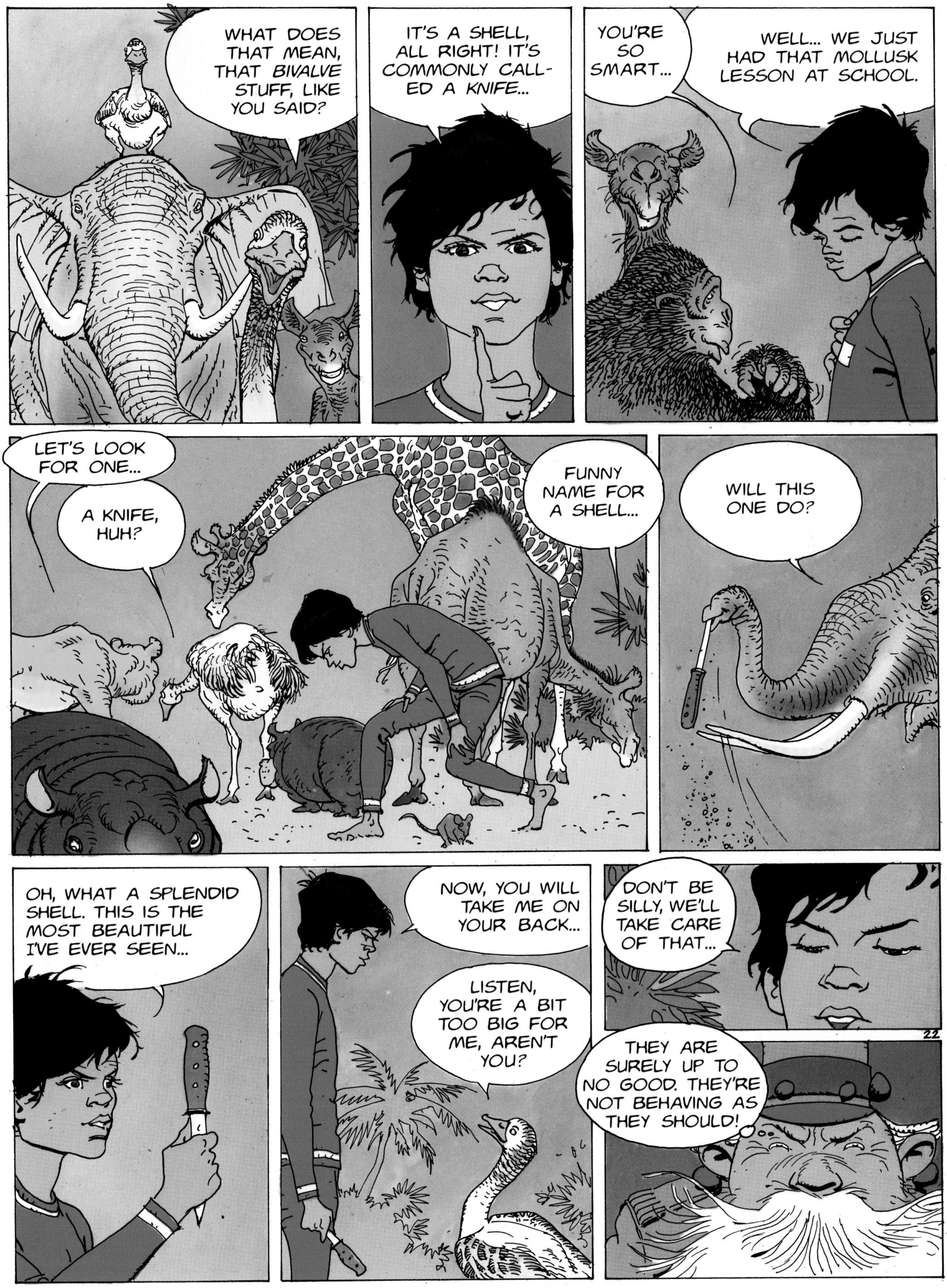
WHAT DOES THAT MEAN, THAT *BIVALVE* STUFF, LIKE YOU SAID?
IT'S A SHELL, ALL RIGHT! IT'S COMMONLY CALL-ED A KNIFE...
YOU'RE SO SMART...
WELL... WE JUST HAD THAT MOLLUSK LESSON AT SCHOOL.
LET'S LOOK FOR ONE...
A KNIFE, HUH?
FUNNY NAME FOR A SHELL...
WILL THIS ONE DO?
OH, WHAT A SPLENDID SHELL. THIS IS THE MOST BEAUTIFUL I'VE EVER SEEN...
NOW, YOU WILL TAKE ME ON YOUR BACK...
LISTEN, YOU'RE A BIT TOO BIG FOR ME, AREN'T YOU?
DON'T BE SILLY, WE'LL TAKE CARE OF THAT...
22
THEY ARE SURELY UP TO NO GOOD. THEY'RE NOT BEHAVING AS THEY SHOULD!

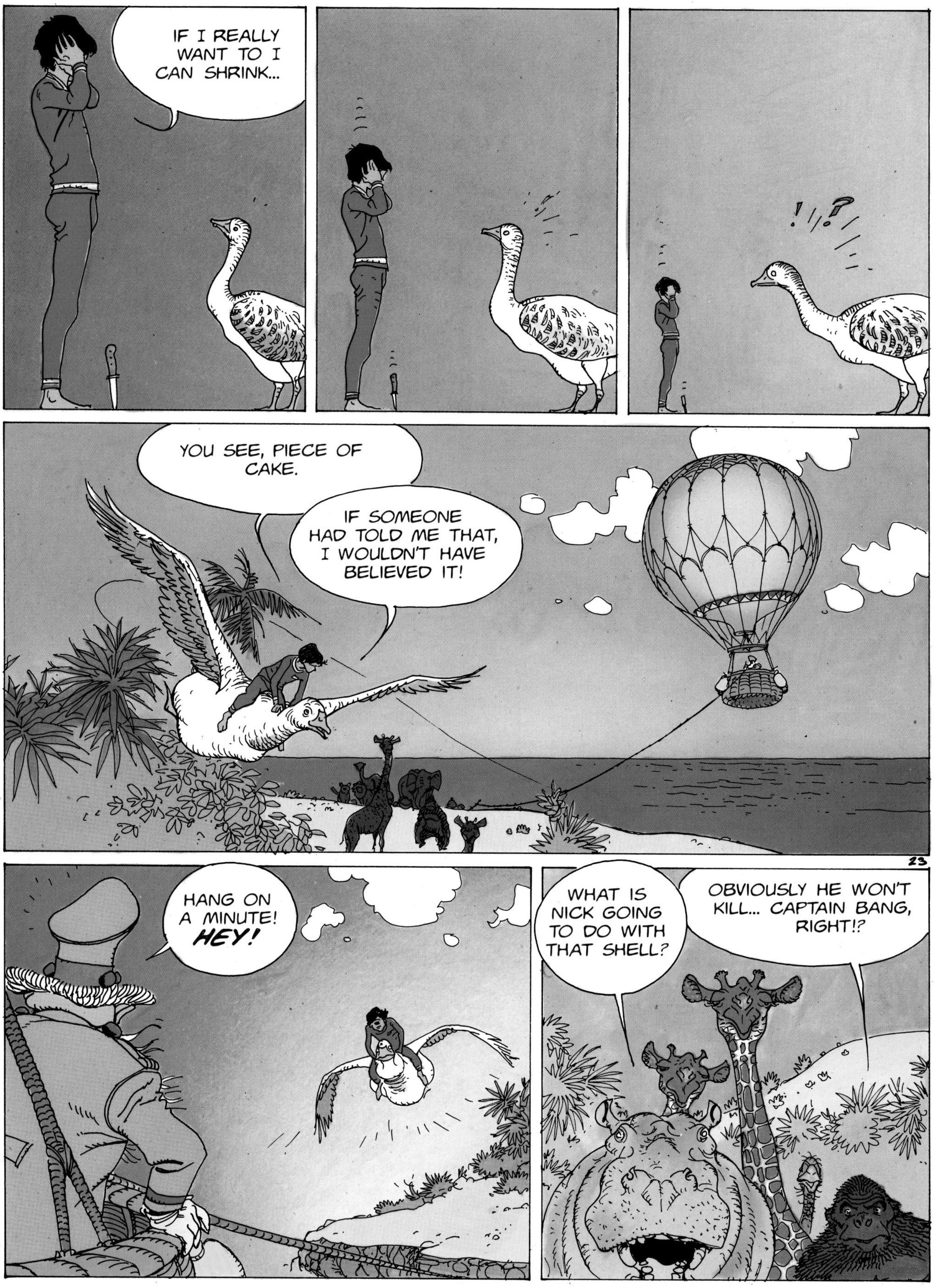
IF I REALLY WANT TO I CAN SHRINK...
YOU SEE, PIECE OF CAKE.
IF SOMEONE HAD TOLD ME THAT, I WOULDN'T HAVE BELIEVED IT!
23
HANG ON A MINUTE! ***HEY!***
WHAT IS NICK GOING TO DO WITH THAT SHELL?
OBVIOUSLY HE WON'T KILL... CAPTAIN BANG, RIGHT!?

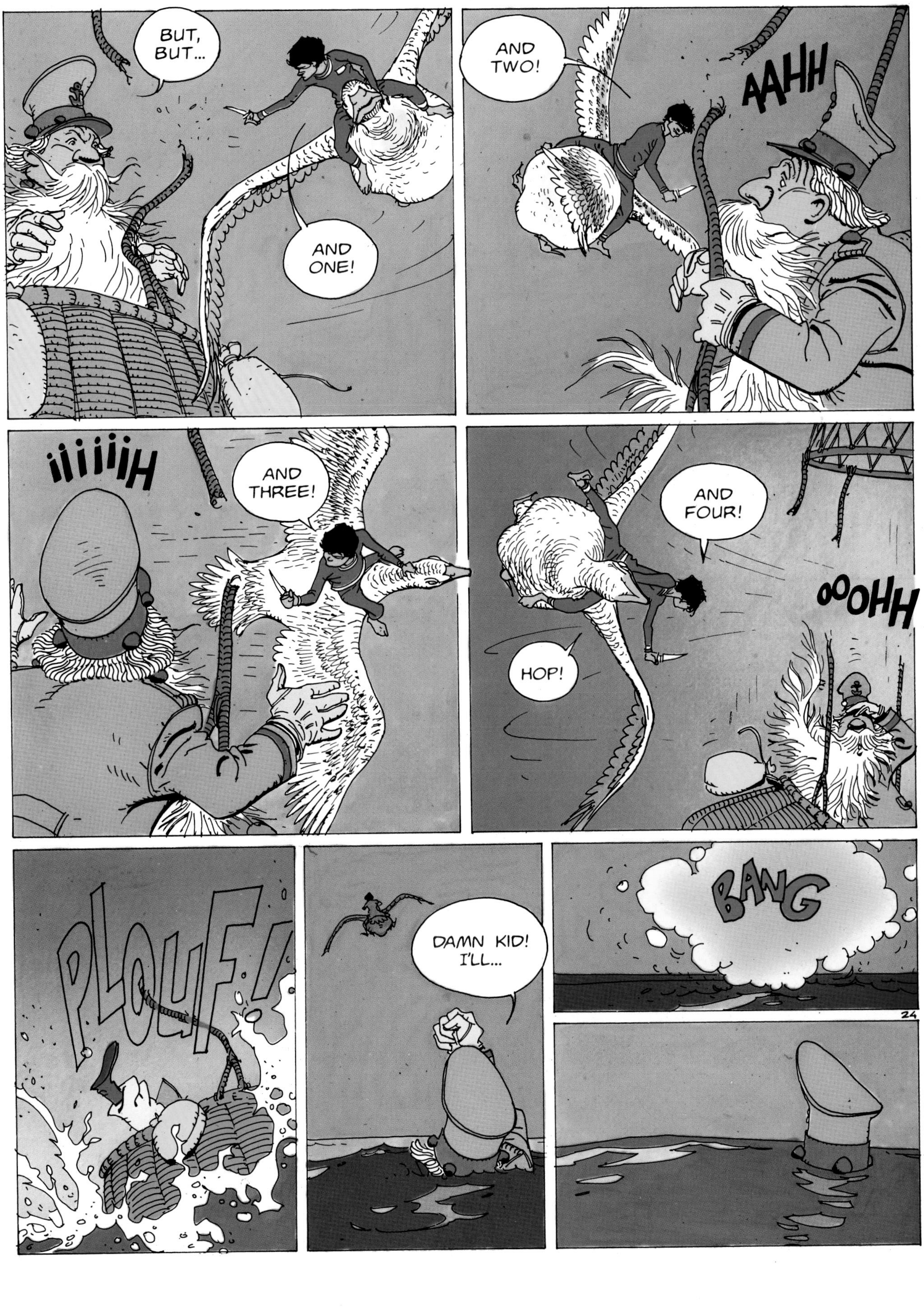
BUT, BUT...
AND ONE!
AND TWO!
AAHH
iiiiiiH
AND THREE!
AND FOUR!
HOP!
OOOHH
PLOUF!!
DAMN KID! I'LL...
BANG
24

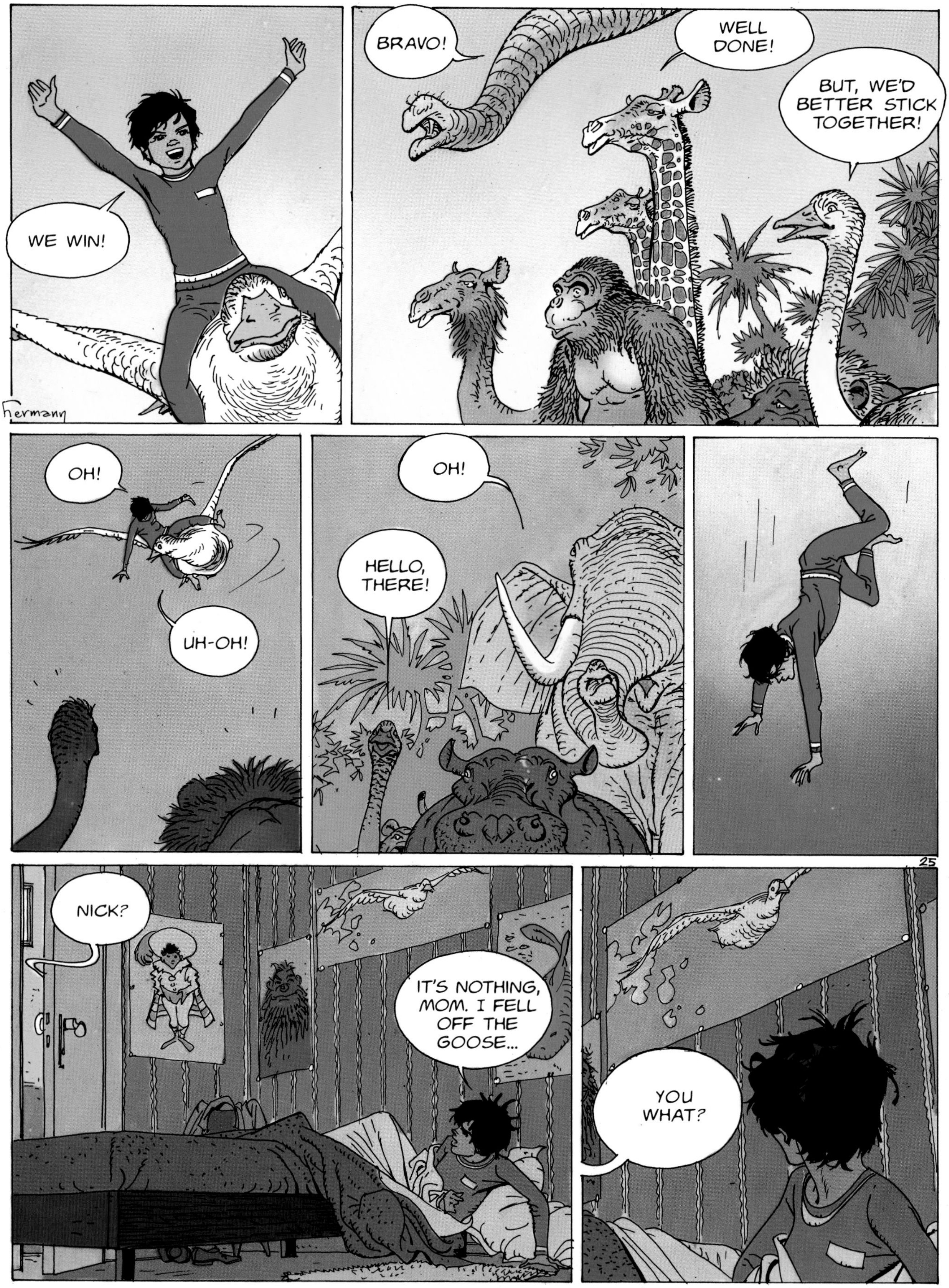

WE WIN!
BRAVO!
WELL DONE!
BUT, WE'D BETTER STICK TOGETHER!
OH!
UH-OH!
OH!
HELLO, THERE!
NICK?
IT'S NOTHING, MOM. I FELL OFF THE GOOSE...
YOU WHAT?

DREAM CHAPTER 4

MOBY DICK AND THE GREAT CACHA

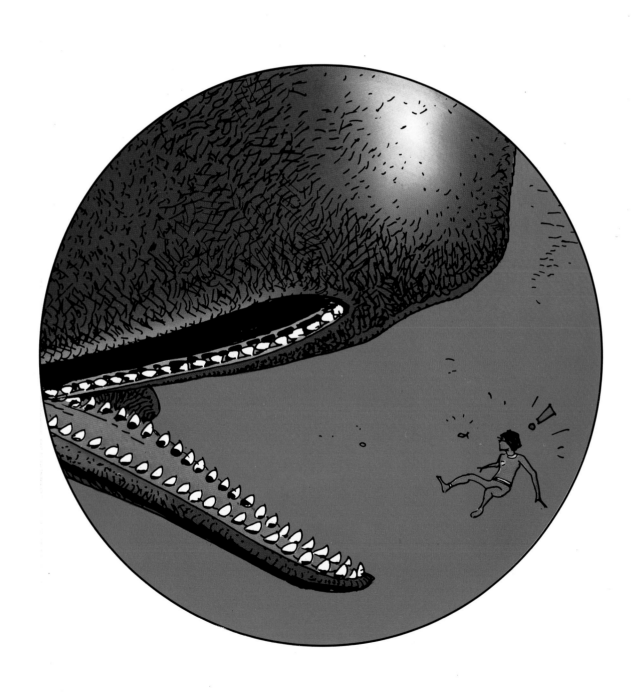

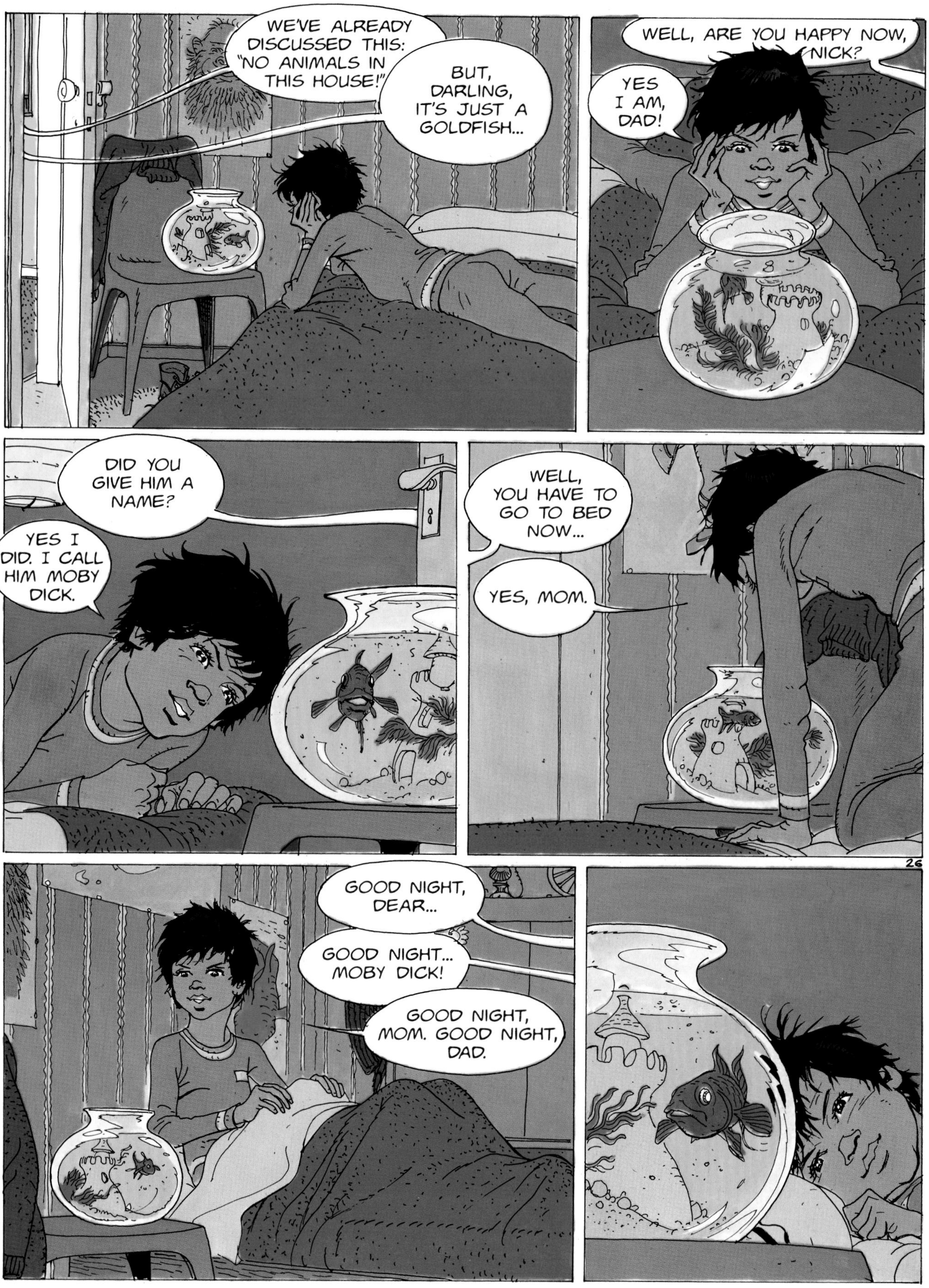
WE'VE ALREADY DISCUSSED THIS: "NO ANIMALS IN THIS HOUSE!"
BUT, DARLING, IT'S JUST A GOLDFISH...
WELL, ARE YOU HAPPY NOW, NICK?
YES I AM, DAD!
DID YOU GIVE HIM A NAME?
YES I DID. I CALL HIM MOBY DICK.
WELL, YOU HAVE TO GO TO BED NOW...
YES, MOM.
26
GOOD NIGHT, DEAR...
GOOD NIGHT... MOBY DICK!
GOOD NIGHT, MOM. GOOD NIGHT, DAD.

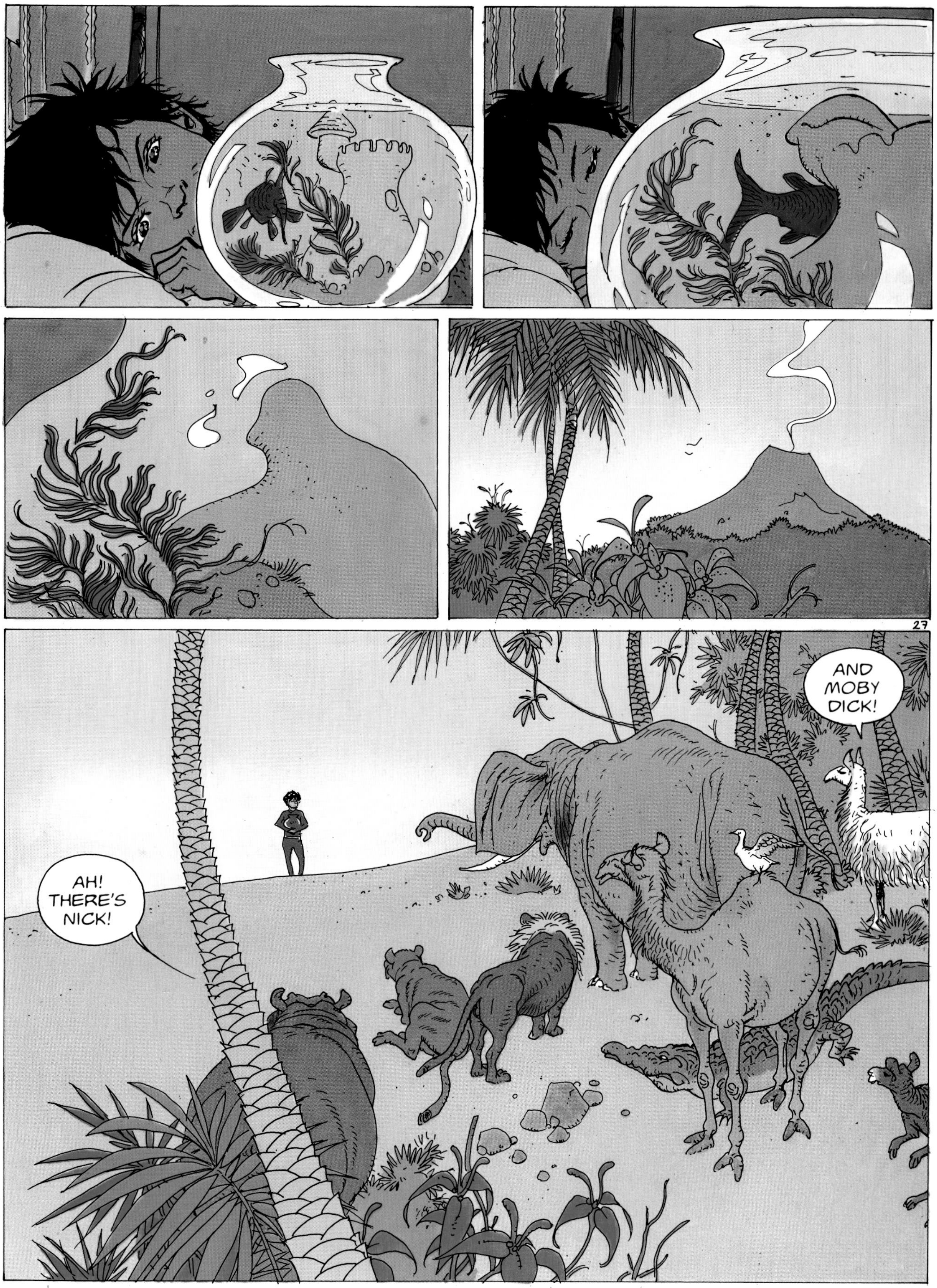
AH! THERE'S NICK!
AND MOBY DICK!

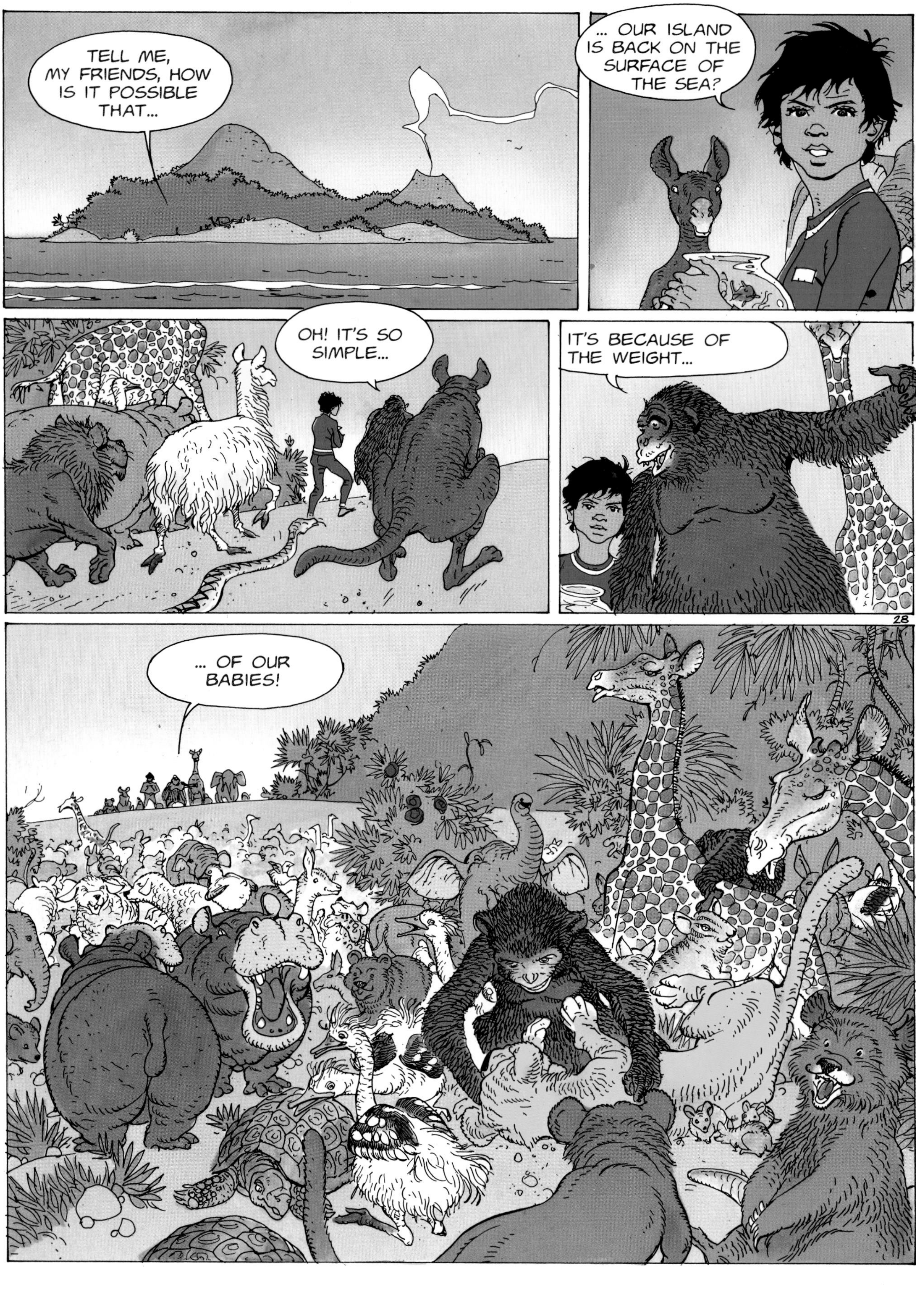
TELL ME, MY FRIENDS, HOW IS IT POSSIBLE THAT...
... OUR ISLAND IS BACK ON THE SURFACE OF THE SEA?
OH! IT'S SO SIMPLE...
IT'S BECAUSE OF THE WEIGHT...
28
... OF OUR BABIES!

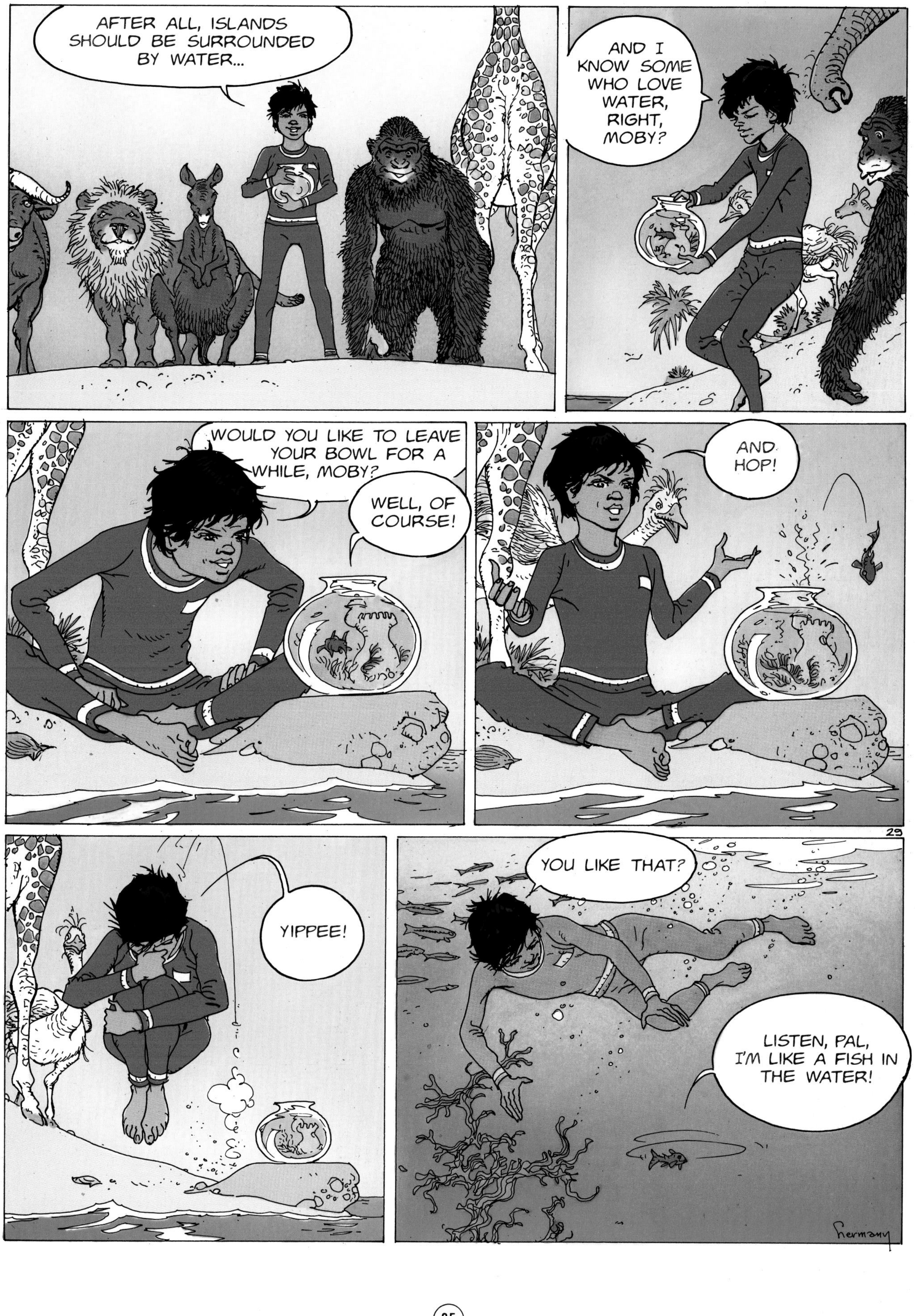
AFTER ALL, ISLANDS SHOULD BE SURROUNDED BY WATER...
AND I KNOW SOME WHO LOVE WATER, RIGHT, MOBY?
WOULD YOU LIKE TO LEAVE YOUR BOWL FOR A WHILE, MOBY?
WELL, OF COURSE!
AND HOP!
29
YIPPEE!
YOU LIKE THAT?
LISTEN, PAL, I'M LIKE A FISH IN THE WATER!
Hermann

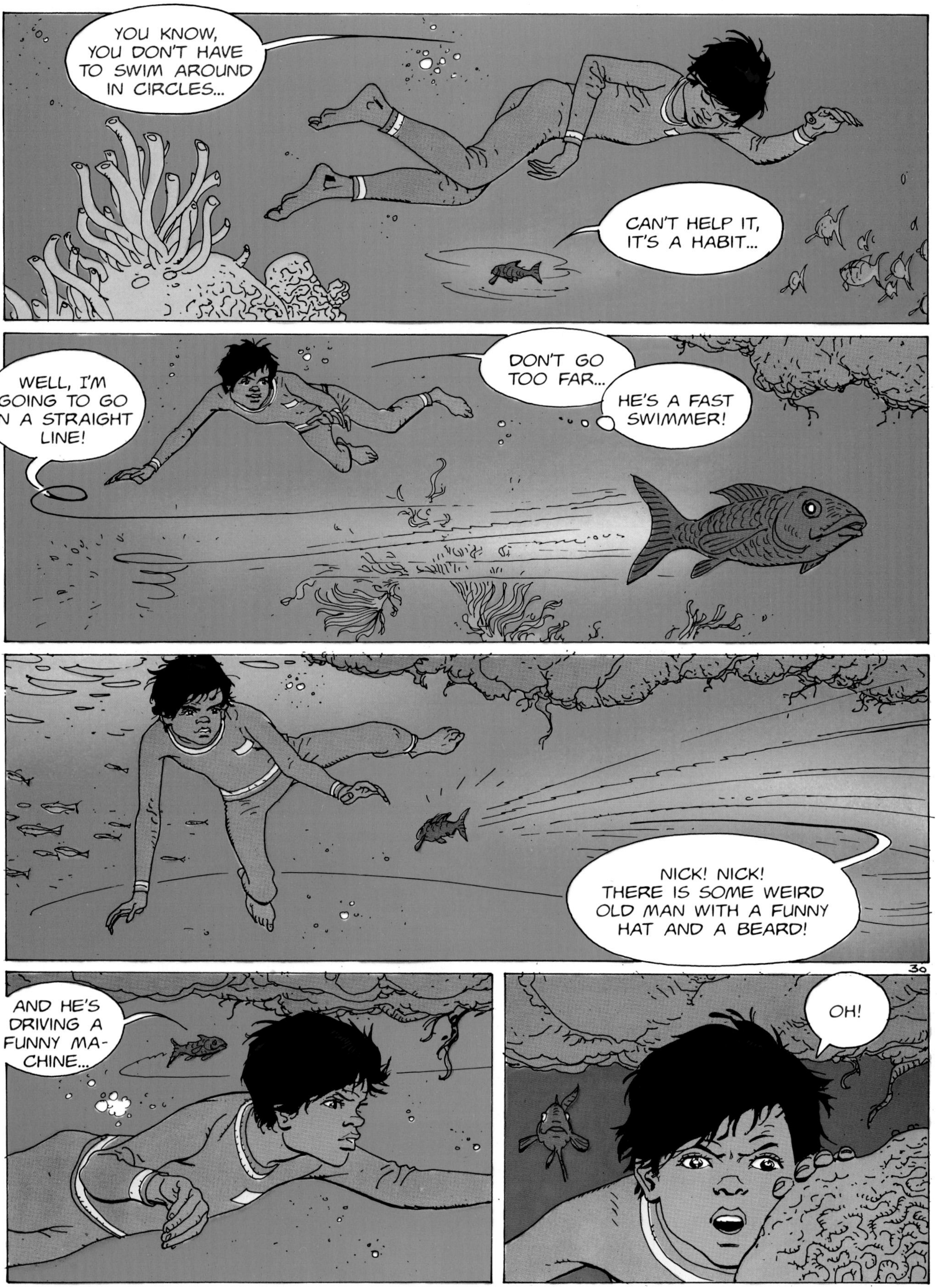
YOU KNOW, YOU DON'T HAVE TO SWIM AROUND IN CIRCLES...
CAN'T HELP IT, IT'S A HABIT...
WELL, I'M GOING TO GO IN A STRAIGHT LINE!
DON'T GO TOO FAR...
HE'S A FAST SWIMMER!
NICK! NICK! THERE IS SOME WEIRD OLD MAN WITH A FUNNY HAT AND A BEARD!
AND HE'S DRIVING A FUNNY MA-CHINE...
OH!

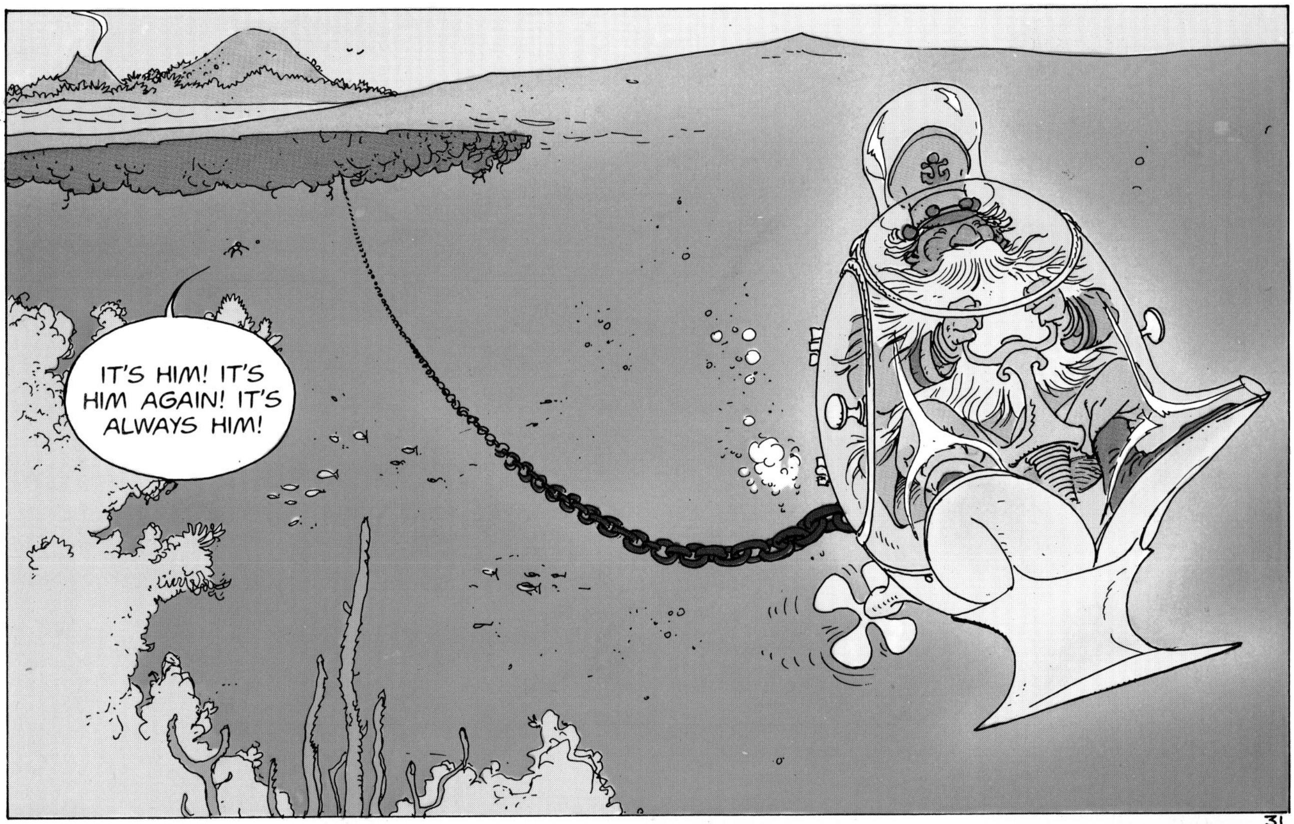
IT'S HIM! IT'S HIM AGAIN! IT'S ALWAYS HIM!

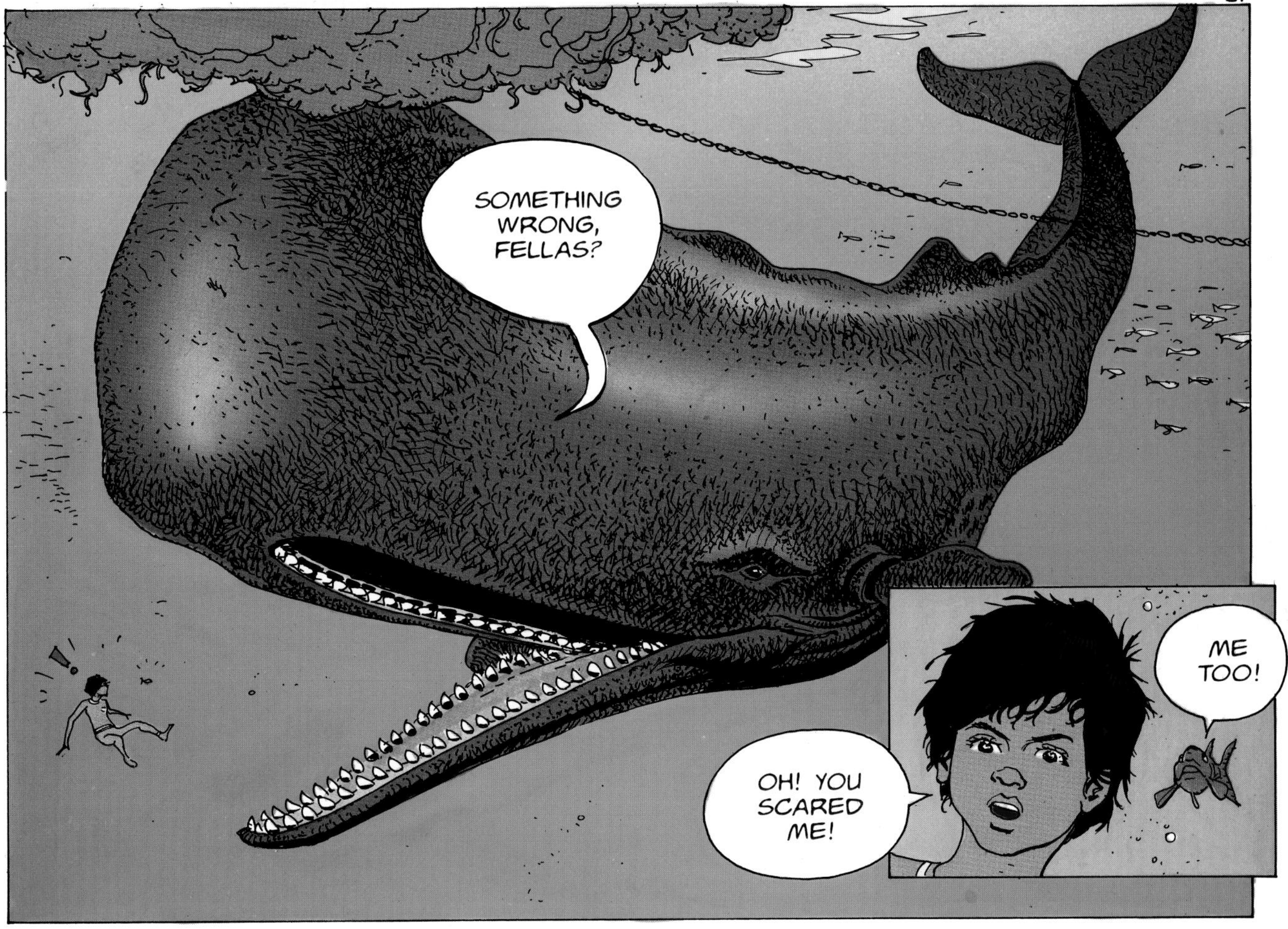
SOMETHING WRONG, FELLAS?
OH! YOU SCARED ME!
ME TOO!

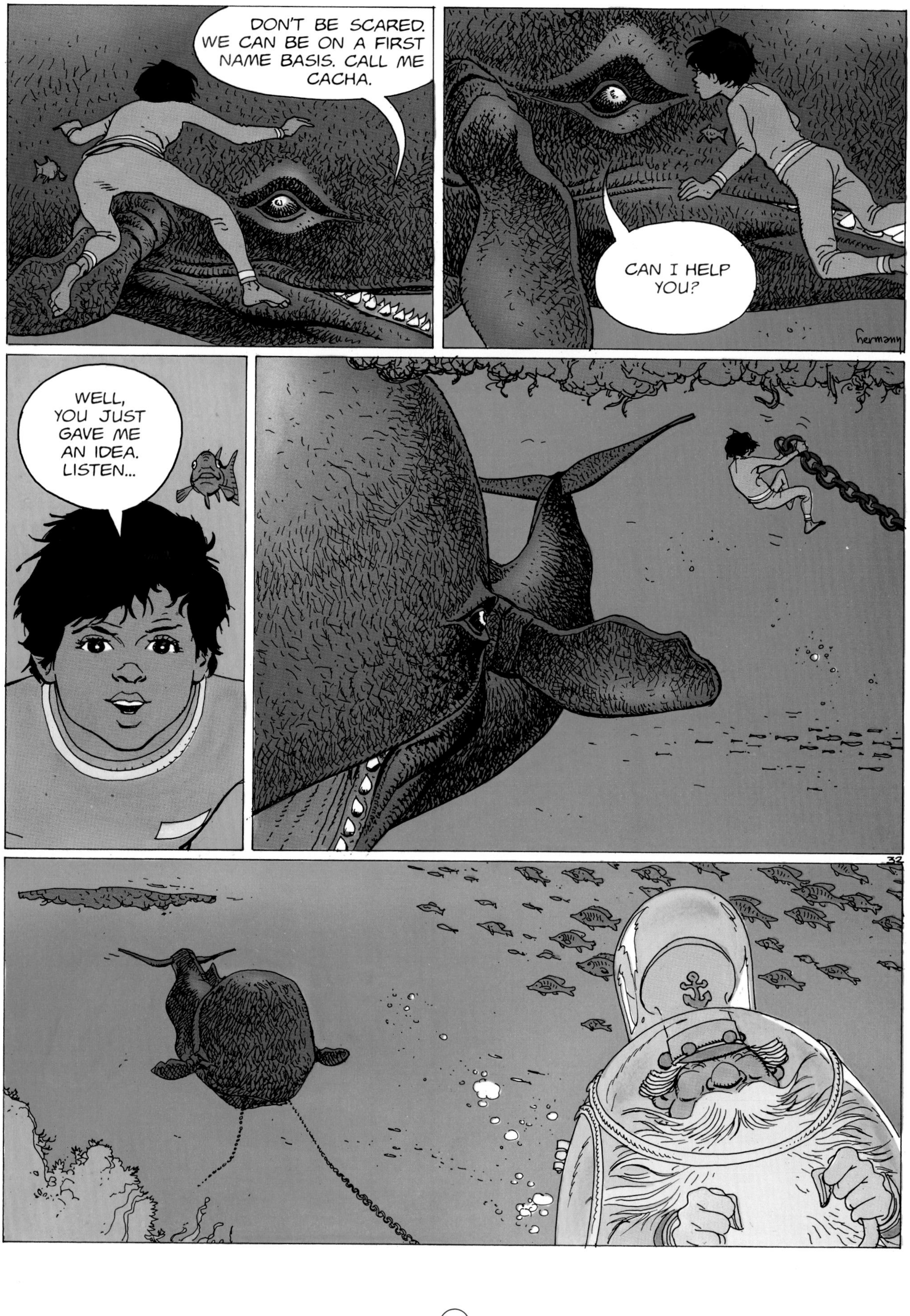
DON'T BE SCARED. WE CAN BE ON A FIRST NAME BASIS. CALL ME CACHA.
CAN I HELP YOU?
hermann
WELL, YOU JUST GAVE ME AN IDEA. LISTEN...
32

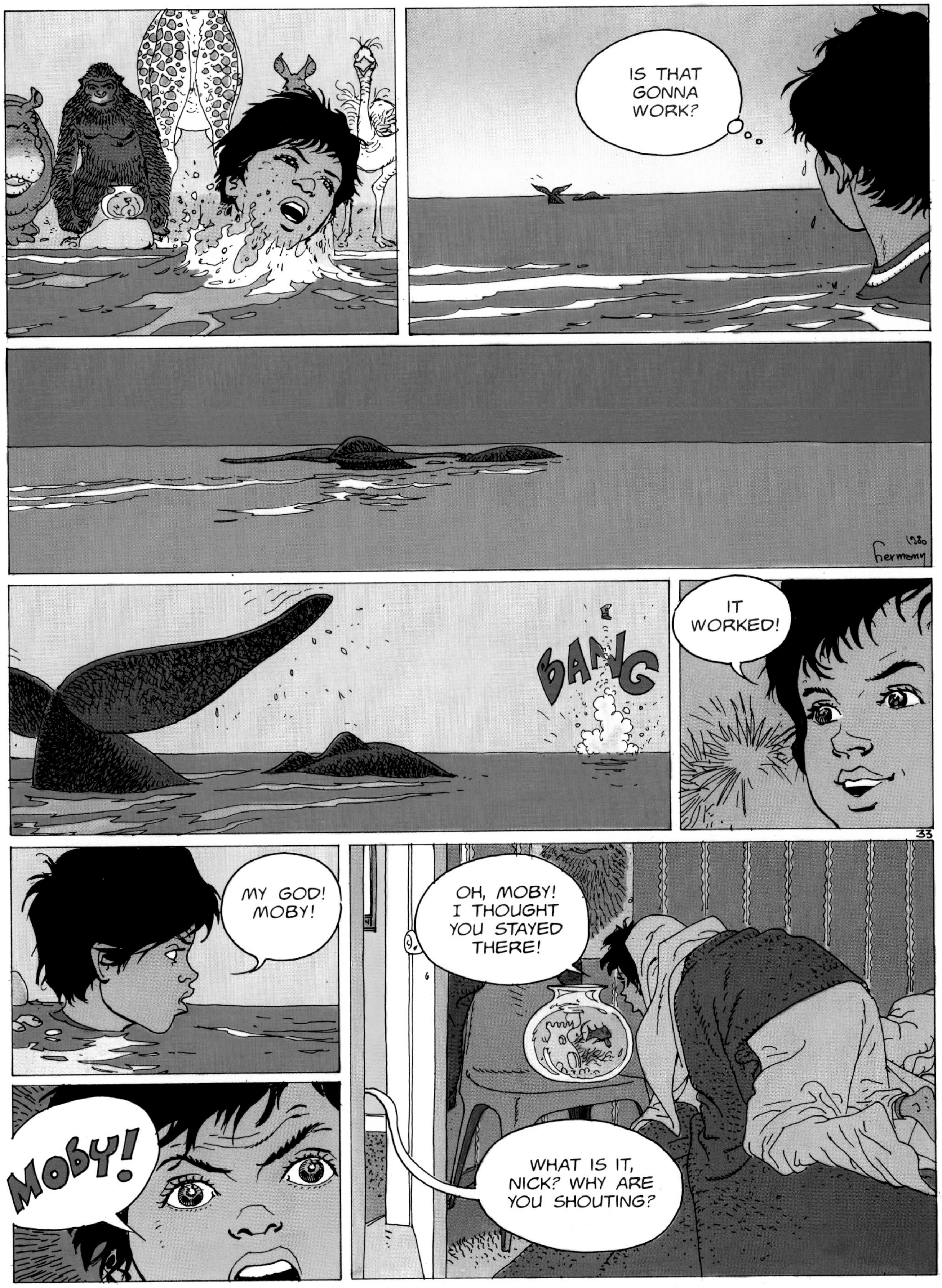
IS THAT GONNA WORK?
BANG
IT WORKED!
MY GOD! MOBY!
OH, MOBY! I THOUGHT YOU STAYED THERE!
MOBY!
WHAT IS IT, NICK? WHY ARE YOU SHOUTING?

DREAM CHAPTER 5

CAPTAIN BANG'S ZOO

COME ON, NICK! IT'S BED-TIME, DEAR!

YES, MOM.

SWEET DREAMS, LITTLE OLD MAN.

YOU'RE IN BED, NICK?

YES, MOM. GOOD NIGHT...

GOOD NIGHT, DEAR.

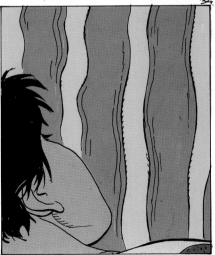

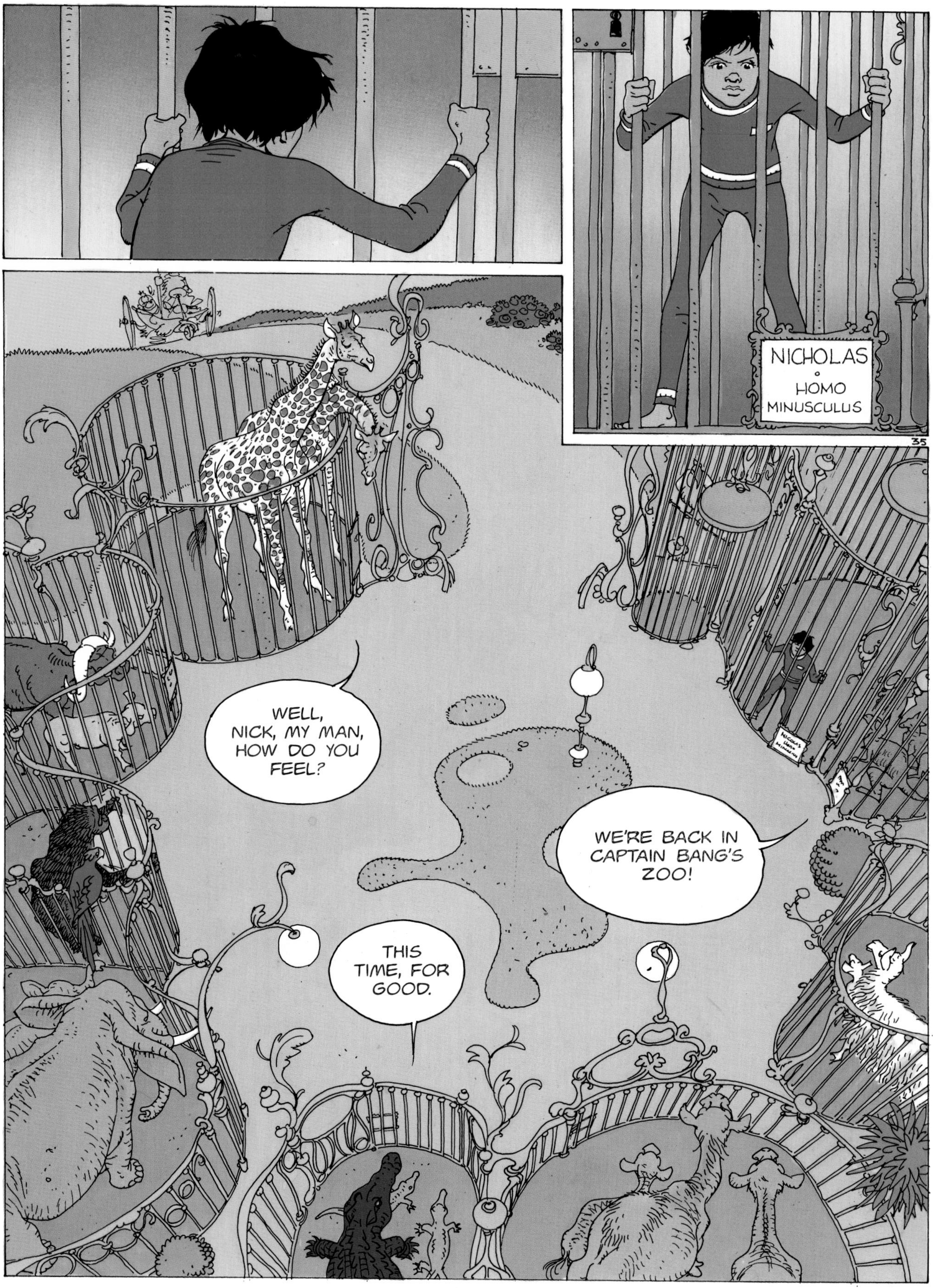
NICHOLAS
HOMO
MINUSCULUS
WELL, NICK, MY MAN, HOW DO YOU FEEL?
WE'RE BACK IN CAPTAIN BANG'S ZOO!
THIS TIME, FOR GOOD.

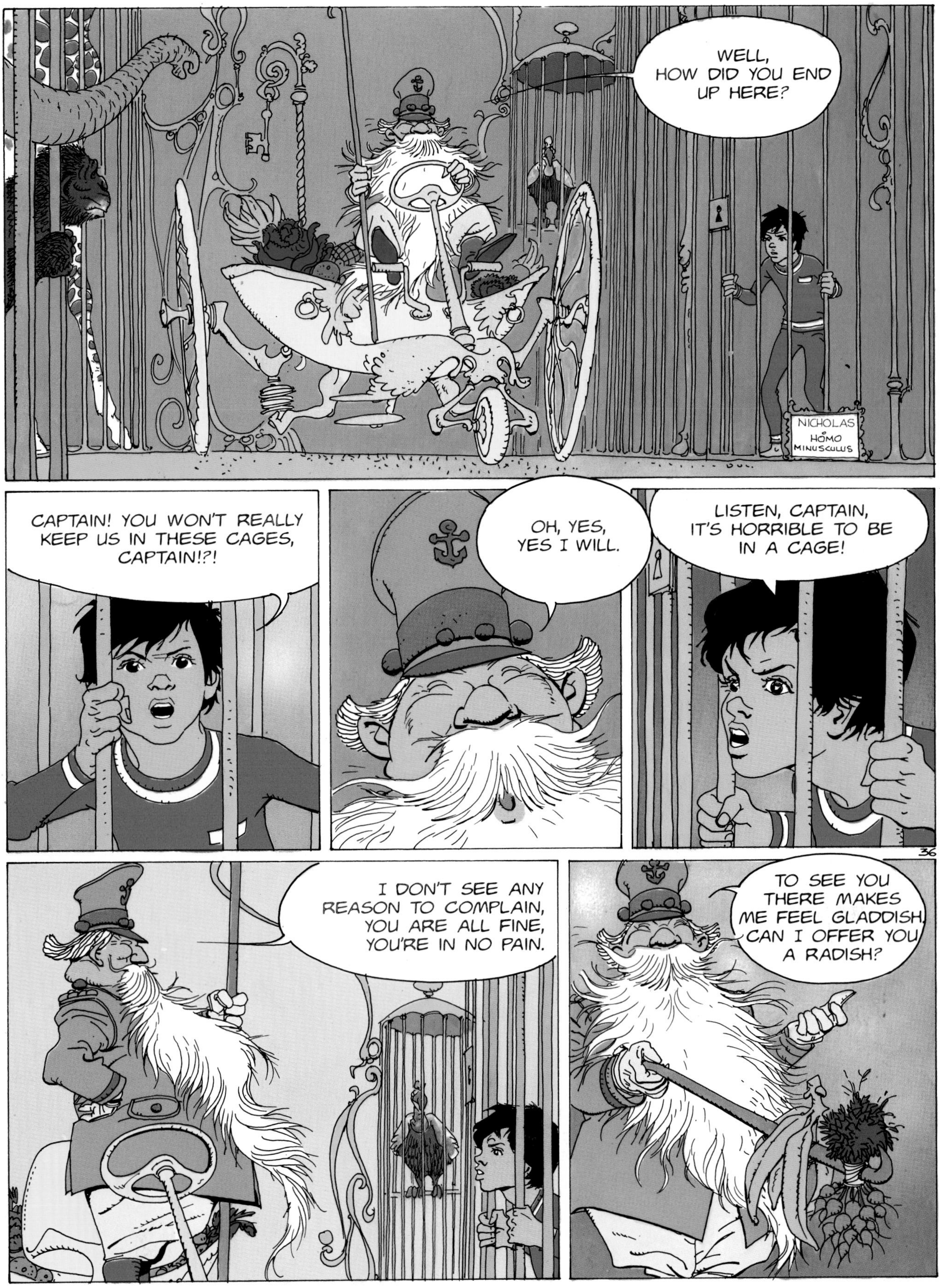
WELL, HOW DID YOU END UP HERE?
NICHOLAS HOMO MINUSCULUS
CAPTAIN! YOU WON'T REALLY KEEP US IN THESE CAGES, CAPTAIN!?!
OH, YES, YES I WILL.
LISTEN, CAPTAIN, IT'S HORRIBLE TO BE IN A CAGE!
36
I DON'T SEE ANY REASON TO COMPLAIN, YOU ARE ALL FINE, YOU'RE IN NO PAIN.
TO SEE YOU THERE MAKES ME FEEL GLADDISH. CAN I OFFER YOU A RADISH?

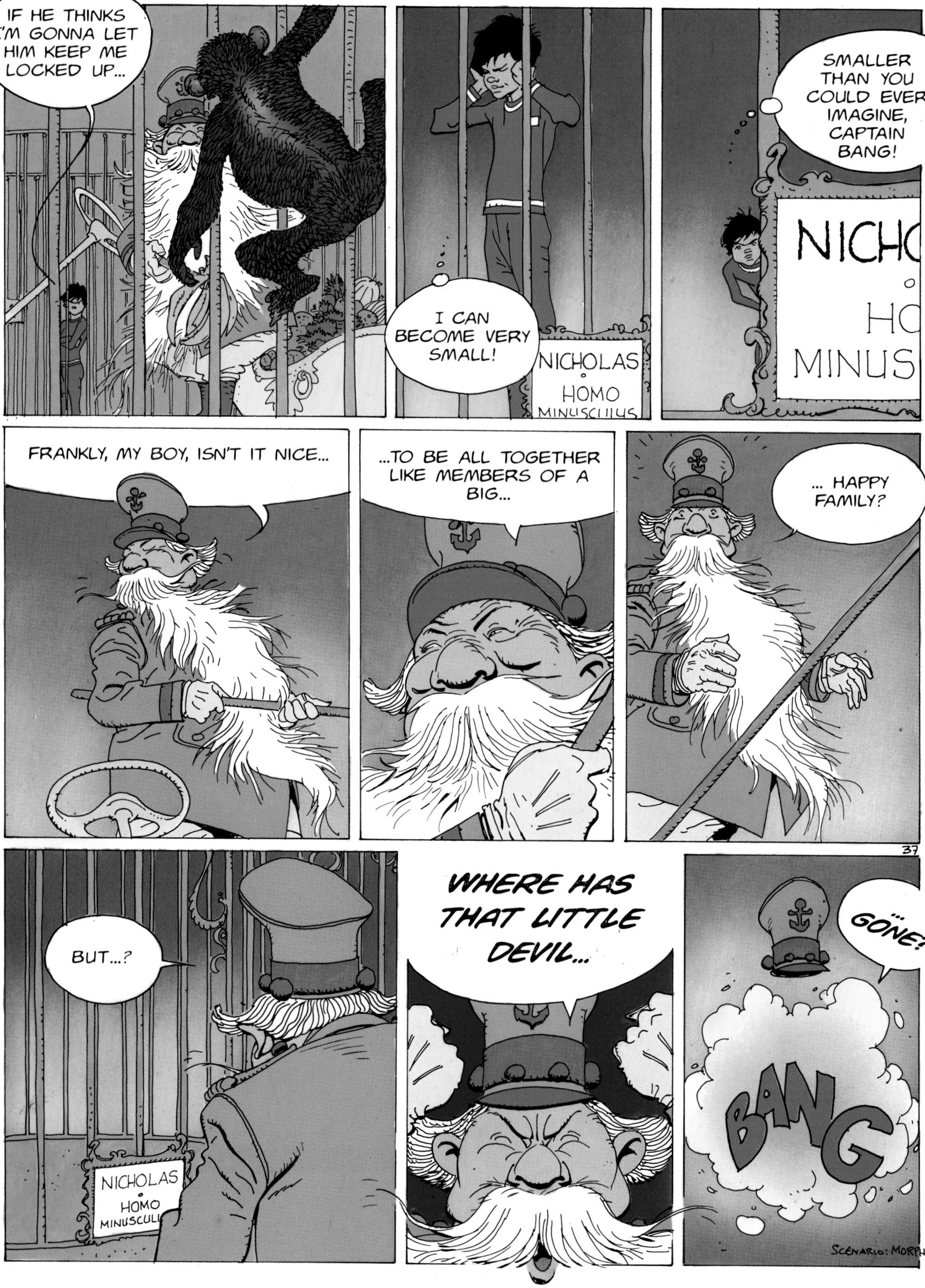
IF HE THINKS I'M GONNA LET HIM KEEP ME LOCKED UP...
I CAN BECOME VERY SMALL!
NICHOLAS
HOMO MINUSCULUS
SMALLER THAN YOU COULD EVER IMAGINE, CAPTAIN BANG!
NICHO
HO
MINUS
FRANKLY, MY BOY, ISN'T IT NICE...
...TO BE ALL TOGETHER LIKE MEMBERS OF A BIG...
... HAPPY FAMILY?
37
BUT...?
NICHOLAS
HOMO MINUSCULI
WHERE HAS THAT LITTLE DEVIL...
... GONE?
BANG
SCÉNARIO: MORPHÉE

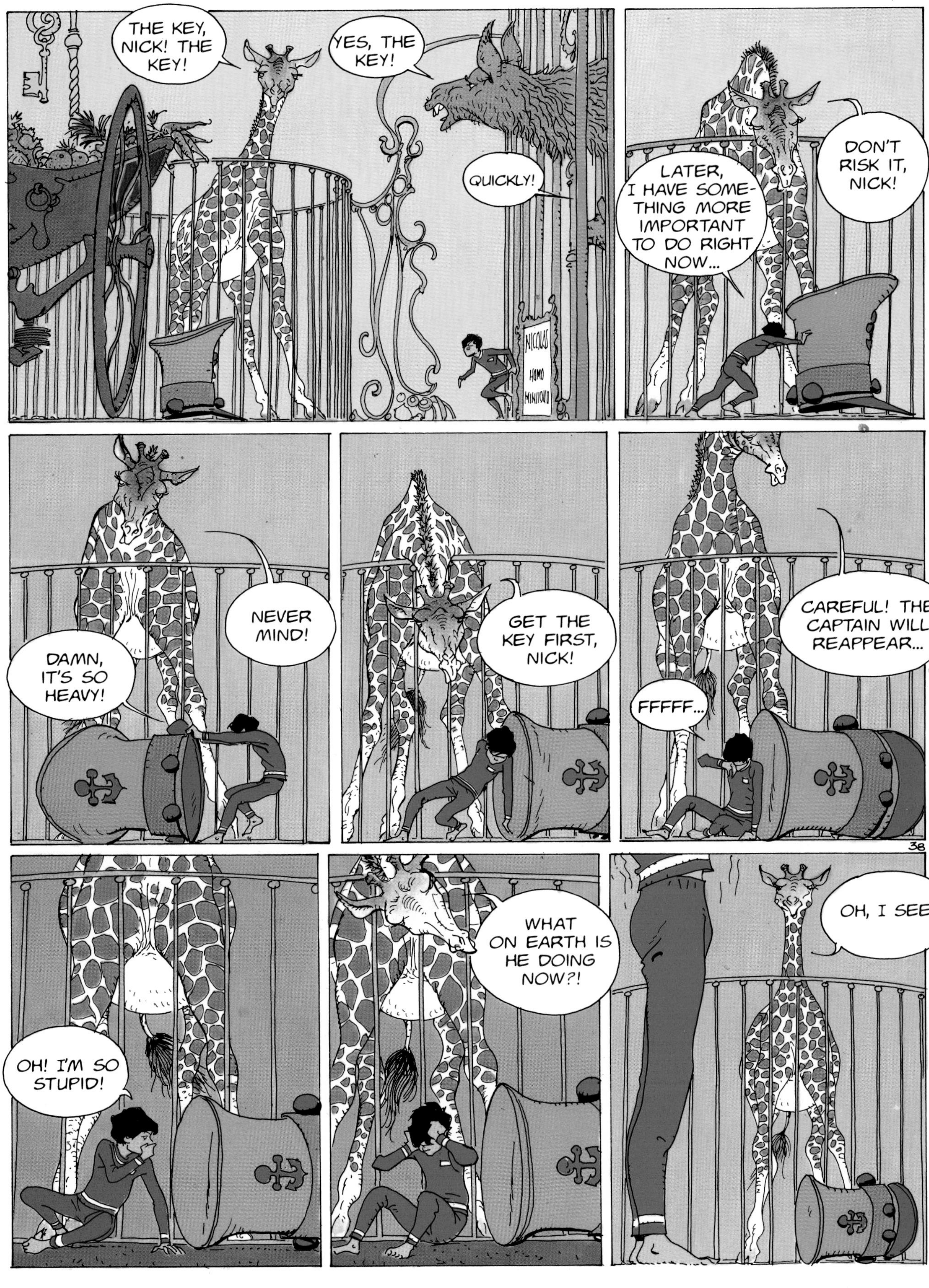
THE KEY, NICK! THE KEY!
YES, THE KEY!
QUICKLY!
LATER, I HAVE SOME-THING MORE IMPORTANT TO DO RIGHT NOW...
DON'T RISK IT, NICK!
NICOLAS HOMO MINIMUS
DAMN, IT'S SO HEAVY!
NEVER MIND!
GET THE KEY FIRST, NICK!
CAREFUL! THE CAPTAIN WILL REAPPEAR...
FFFFF...
OH! I'M SO STUPID!
WHAT ON EARTH IS HE DOING NOW?!
OH, I SEE!

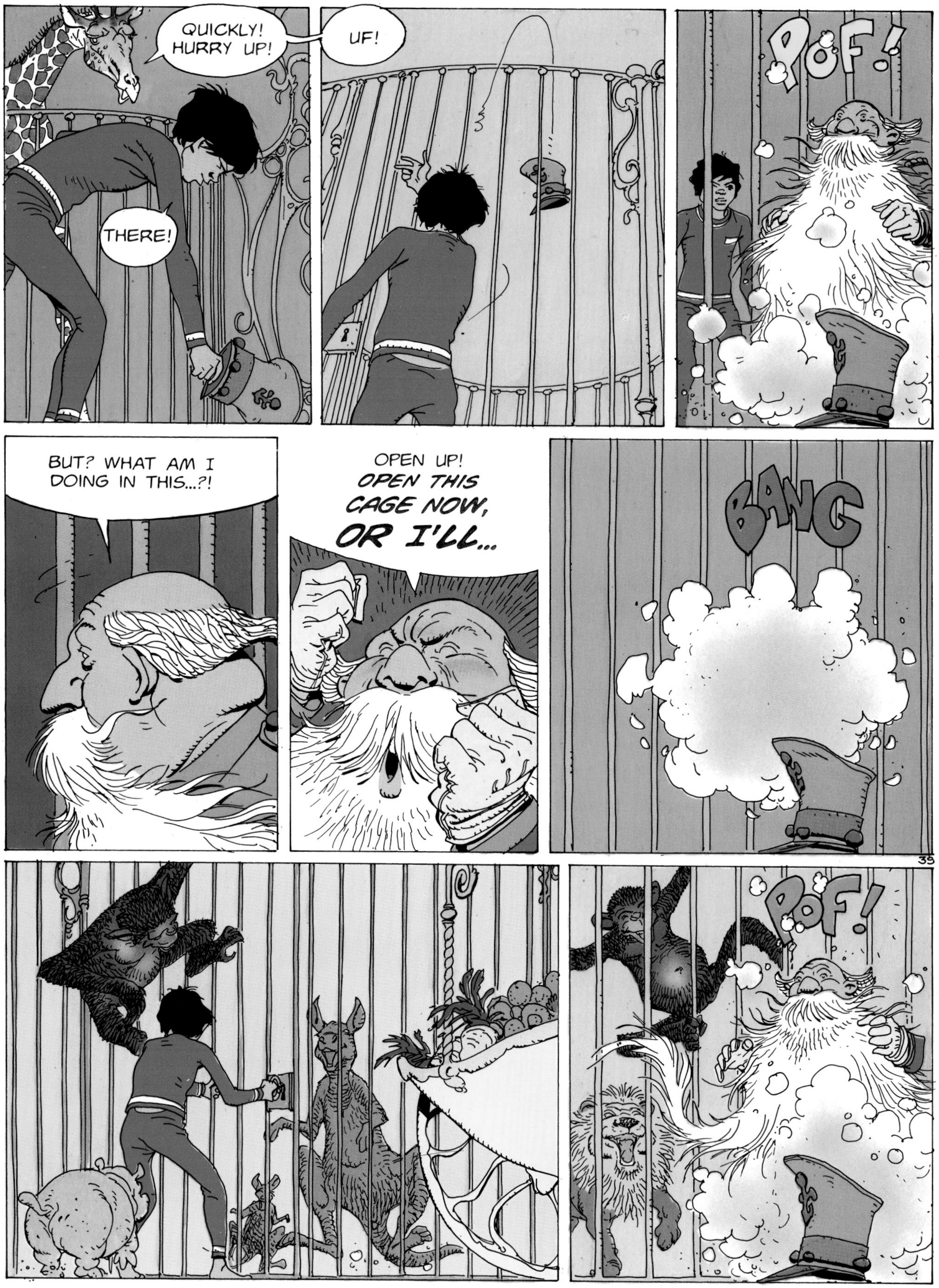
QUICKLY! HURRY UP!
UF!
THERE!
POF!
BUT? WHAT AM I DOING IN THIS...?!
OPEN UP! OPEN THIS CAGE NOW, OR I'LL...
BANG
POF!

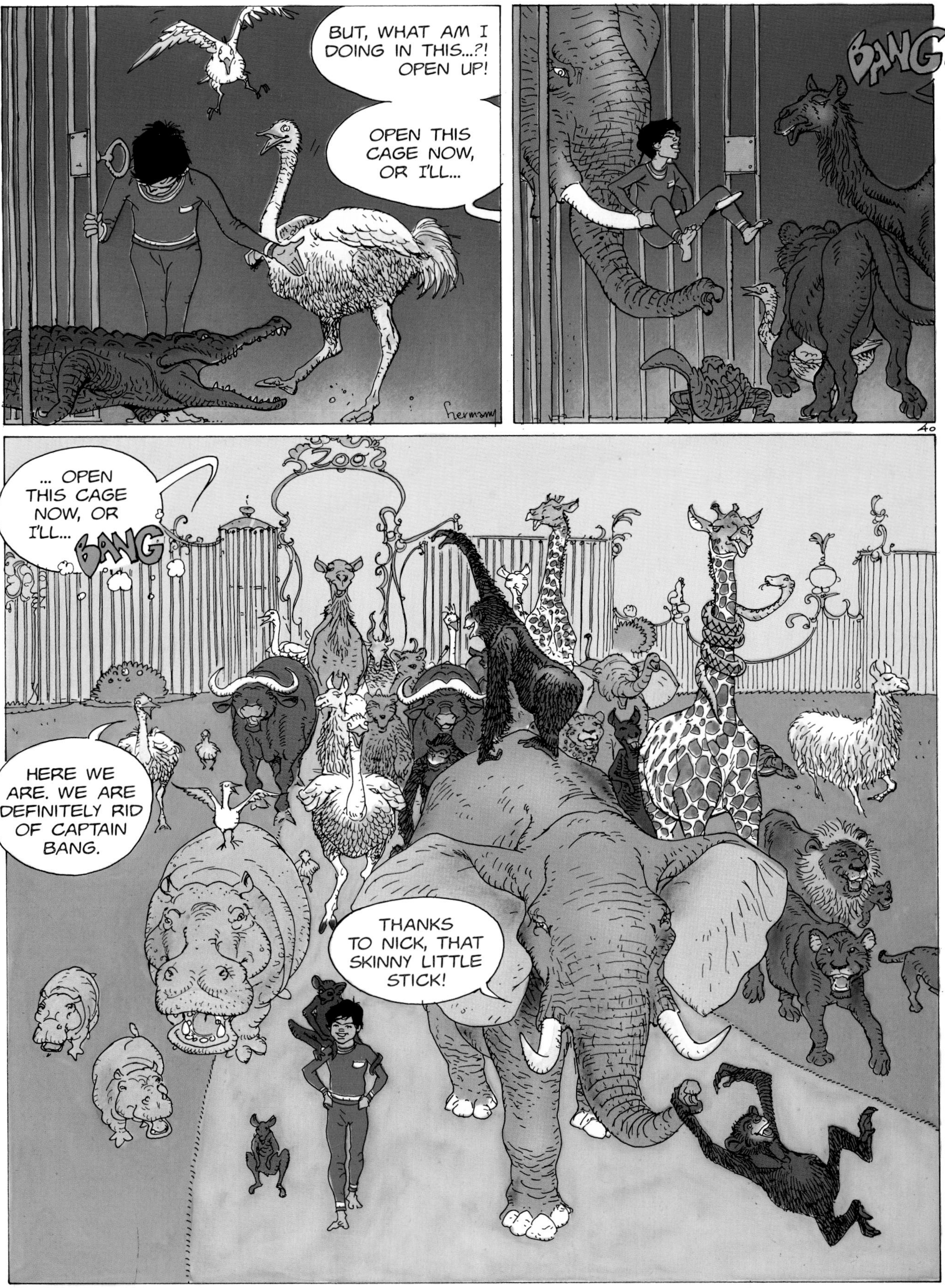
BUT, WHAT AM I DOING IN THIS...?! OPEN UP!
OPEN THIS CAGE NOW, OR I'LL...
BANG!
ZOO
... OPEN THIS CAGE NOW, OR I'LL... BANG
HERE WE ARE. WE ARE DEFINITELY RID OF CAPTAIN BANG.
THANKS TO NICK, THAT SKINNY LITTLE STICK!

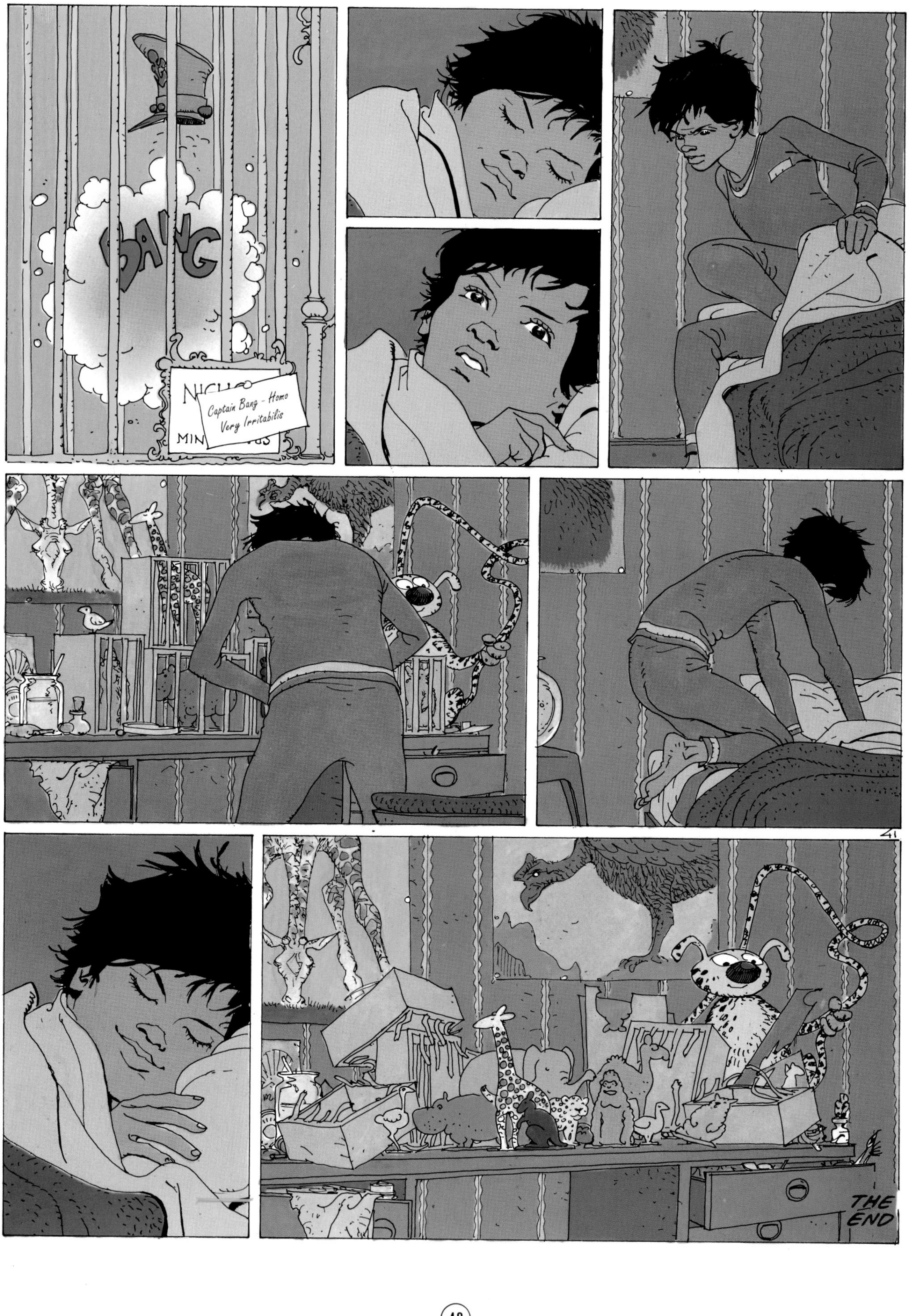
BANG
Captain Bang - Homo
Very Irritabilis
THE END

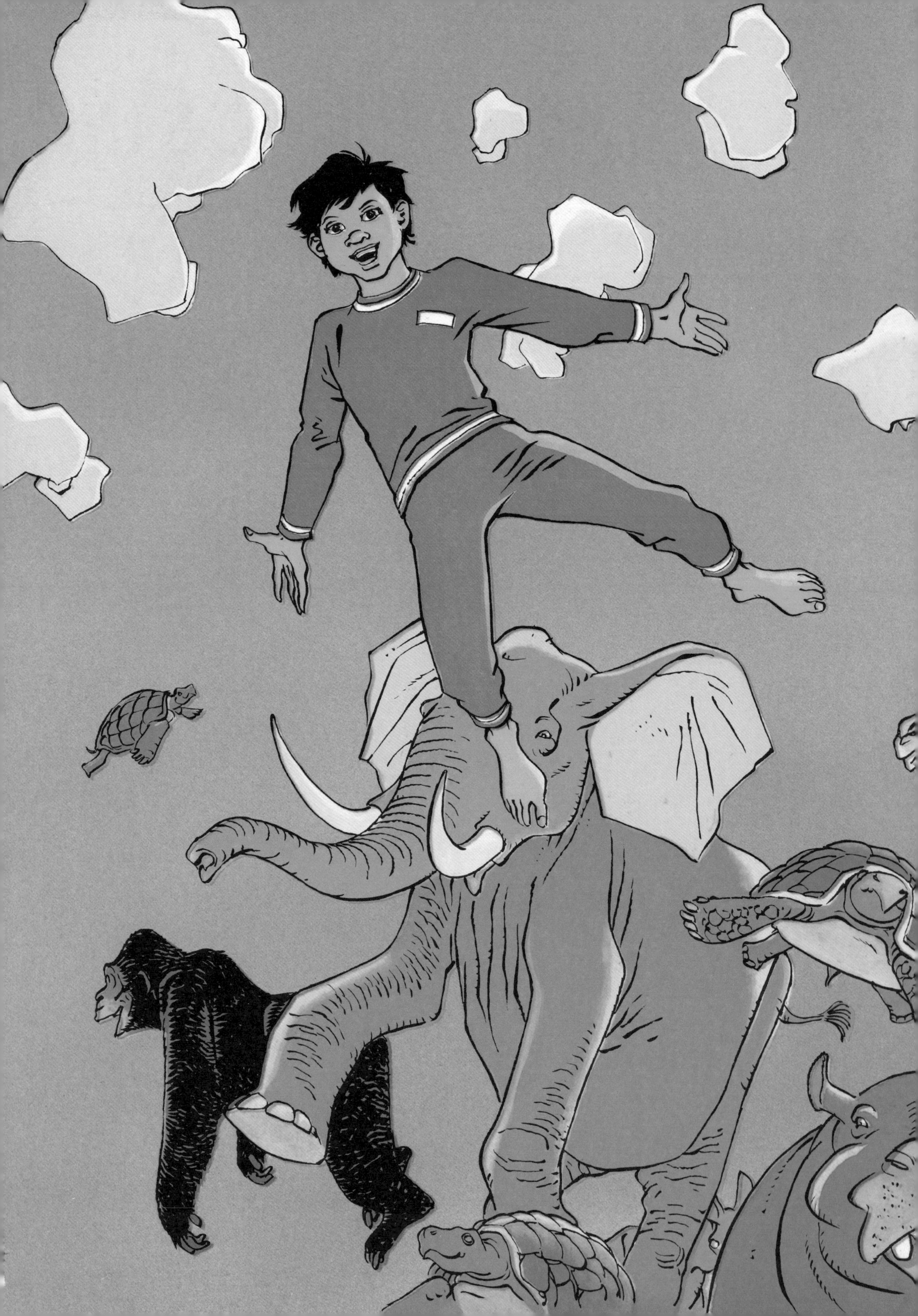